IMAGES OF WAR
NAVAL AVIATION IN THE SECOND WORLD WAR

RARE PHOTOGRAPHS FROM WARTIME ARCHIVES

PHILIP KAPLAN

Pen & Sword
AVIATION

First printed in Great Britain in 2013
Pen & Sword Aviation
an imprint of
Pen & Sword Books Ltd.
47 Church Street
Barnsley,
South Yorkshire
S70 2AS

A CIP record for this book is available from the British Library

ISBN 978 1 78159 369 1

Printed and bound in England
By CPI Group (UK) Ltd. Croydon, CRO 4YY

Pen & Sword Books Ltd incorporates the Imprints of Pen & Sword Aviation, Pen & Sword Family History, Pen & Sword Maritime, Pen & Sword Military, Pen & Sword Discovery, Wharncliffe Local History, Wharncliffe True Crime, Wharncliffe Transport, Pen & Sword Select, Pen & Sword Military Classics, Leo Cooper, The Praetorian Press, Remember When, Seaforth Publishing and Frontline Publishing.

For a complete list of Pen & Sword titles please contact
Pen & Sword Books Limited
47 Church Street, Barnsley, South Yorkshire, S70 2AS
England

E-mail: enquiries@pen-and-sword.co.uk
Website: www.pen-and-sword.co.uk

Contents

Photographs from the collections of the author. Reasonable efforts have been made to trace the copyright owners of all material used in this book. The author apologizes to any copyright owners we were unable to contact during this clearance process. All reasonable efforts will be made to correct such omissions in future editions. The author is grateful to the following for the use of their published and/or unpublished material, or for their kind and generous assitance in the preparation of this book: Malcolm Bates, John Bolt, Jennifer Brattle, Eric Brown, James Cain, Shannon Callahan, Larry Cauble, Ed Copeland, Bob Croman, Dale Dean, Robert Elder, Frank Furbish, Tess and George Gay, Jack Glass Stephen Grey, Christy Sheaff-Hagen, Chris Hurst, Imperial War Museum, Kelly Kinsella, Jack Kleiss, Alan Leahy, Paul Ludwig, Richard May, Richard McCutcheon, Hamilton McWhorter, Morris Montgomery, H.B. Moranville, Jeff Mulkey, Bruce Porter, Royal Navy, Henry Sakaida, Doug Siegfried, David Smith, Mark Stanhope, Danny Stembridge, David Tarry, Mark Thistlethwaite, U.S. Navy, Stanley Vejtasa, Danny Vincent, Alex Vraciu, Nigel Ward, Sky Webb, Wilbur Webb, John Wellham, Dennis Wrynn, Aaron Zizzo, HMS *Illustrious*, USS *John C. Stennis*.

The First Flattops

An aircraft carrier is a noble thing. It lacks almost everything that seems to denote nobility, yet deep nobility is there. A carrier has no poise. It has no grace. It is top-heavy and lop-sided. It has the lines of a well-fed cow. It doesn't cut through the water like a cruiser, knifing romantically along. It doesn't dance and cavort like a destroyer. It just plows. You feel it should be carrying a hod, rather than wearing a red sash. Yet a carrier is a ferocious thing, and out of its heritage of action has grown nobility. I believe that today every navy in the world has as its number one priority the destruction of enemy carriers. That's a precarious honor, but it's a proud one.
—Ernie Pyle, war correspondent, World War II

The first aircraft carriers made their appearance in the early years of World War One. These first flat-tops were improvised affairs built on hulls that had been laid down with other purposes in mind, and it was not until the 1920s that the first purpose-built carriers were launched, but no one was as yet clear about the role of the carriers and they were largely unloved by the "battleship admirals" who still believed that their great dreadnoughts were the ultimate capital ships.

The centenary of naval aviation was celebrated in 2011 in remembrance of the pioneering efforts and sacrifices of people like Eugene Ely, an exhibition pilot for aircraft designer and builder Glenn Curtiss. Ely had worked as a chauffeur and then as a salesman for Portland, Oregon auto dealer Harry Wemme who had purchased a Curtiss biplane and then become an agent for Curtiss products. Wemme, however, was afraid to fly and Ely offered to try and fly the plane for him. He crashed the plane and, embarrassed by the accident, bought the wreck from Wemme, repaired it and within a month taught himself to fly. He bagan making appearances at various air meets and at one such event in Minneapolis, he met Glenn Curtiss and some of his associates. Ely also happened to meet Captain Washington Chambers, USN, who had been appointed by Secretary of the Navy George Meyer to investigate military uses for aviation within the Navy. The meeting led to experiments by Ely with a Curtiss Pusher aircraft. He made the world's first reasonably successful take-off in a fixed-wing plane from the deck

below: HMS *Eagle*; right: HMS *Argus*

of a ship. In November 1910, he flew a Curtiss Pusher down a gently sloping wooden platform on the forecastle of the light cruiser USS *Birmingham* as the ship steamed slowly in Hampton Roads, Chesapeake Bay, Virginia, In the brief flight, Ely's plane actually touched the water when it plunged downward after clearing the eighty-three-foot platform runway, but he managed to retain control and landed safely on the shore at Willoughby Spit, rather than circling the harbour and landing at the Norfolk Navy Yard as planned. On the following January 11th, Ely, wearing a padded football helmet and a bicycle tube as a survival vest, took off from the site of what became the Tanforan race track in San Bruno, California, his aircraft equipped with a system of grappling hooks fitted underneath the air-foil that caught arresting wires attached to sandbags. The system was devised and built by circus per-former and aviator Hugh Robinson, and Ely successfully landed the Curtiss Pusher at forty mph aboard a platform on the USS *Pennsylvania* then anchored in San Francisco Bay. When interviewed after the feat, Ely told a news reporter: "It was easy enough. I think the trick could be successfully turned nine times out of ten." Ely continued flying exhibitions for Curtiss and when asked by a reporter for the Des Moines Register if he had any plans for retiring, he replied: "I guess I will be like the rest of them, keep at it until I am killed." In October 1911, just before what would have been his twenty-fifth birth-day, Eugene Ely was killed in the crash of an aircraft he was displaying at Macon, Georgia. In 1933, the U.S. Congress awarded Ely a posthumous Distinguished Flying Cross "for extraordinary achievement as a pioneer civilian aviator and for his significant contribution to the development of aviation in the United States Navy."

Britain, for her part, counts 2009 as the centenary year of naval aviation, as it was in 1909 that the Admiralty designated the then grand sum of £35,000 toward development of an airship and the process that began the formation of the Fleet Air Arm. The nation chose to celebrate the anniversary year with a programme of events and publications commemorating the centenary and showcasing the endurance, flexibility, and the potency of naval aviation.

In December 1910, Glenn Curtiss offered—at his own expense—to "instruct an officer of the United States Navy in the operation and construction of a Curtiss aeroplane, and on 23 December Lieutenant T. G. Ellyson reported for instruction at North Island, San Diego Bay. Four months later he was graduated by Curtiss who wrote to the Secretary of the Navy: "Lt. Ellyson is now competent to

far left: HMS *Courageous* at sea; left: HMS *Ark Royal*; below: HMS *Courageous* which was initially a cruiser and then rebuilt as an aircraft carrier in the mid-1920s.

care for and operate Curtiss aeroplanes." Ellyson became America's first naval aviator. In Great Britain, Commander Charles R. Samson, RN, achieved the first fixed-wing aircraft take-off from a moving warship on 9 May 1912 when his Short S.38 rose from the battleship HMS *Hibernia* while she was steaming at seventeen mph during the Royal Fleet Review at Weymouth.

The brothers Orville and Wilbur Wright had made their initial powered flight at Kitty Hawk on the coast of North Carolina in December 1903, and less than eight years later men were demonstrating the ability to take off from and, with the aid of arresting wires, recover an aircraft to a "carrier deck" of a ship. That ability, tied to the value and significance of aviation for reconnaissance and patrol purposes, pursuaded the U. S. Navy that aircraft carriers or "floating airports" must be designed, developed and acquired in order to exploit and support its combat aeroplanes. The British, though, were at the forefront of such development and, by 1913, had identified and defined virtually all of the most fundamental needs of carrier operation, aircraft and equipment. Their HMS *Ark Royal*, laid down initially as a merchant ship and then converted in her building stocks to a hybrid aeroplane/seaplane carrier with a launch platform, was arguably the first modern aircraft carrier. *Ark Royal* served in the Dardanellles campaign and through the First World War.

The British led the navies of the world in bomb-dropping, gun mounting and firing, and the development and successful launching of a fourteen-inch torpedo, as well as wing-folding for the improved stowage of bulky aircraft in the limited space of a ship deck. The British had soon decided that it was

left: Built for the Royal Navy during the First World War, HMS *Furious* was largely a work in progress paving the way for the next British aircraft carriers; right: HMS *Glorious* was originally a *Courageous* class battle-cruiser, rebuilt as an aircraft carrier in the 1920s. After supporting British operations in Norway during April 1940, she was sunk by the German battlecruisers *Scharnhorst* and *Gneisenau* two months later.

essential to develop the purpose-built aircraft carrier, something they achieved by the end of the First World War. The Royal Navy and the navies of France, Japan, and the United States were then hard at the task of converting existing vessels to become aircraft carriers. The Americans followed the British lead, in converting the collier *Jupiter* into an experimental aircraft carrier they recommissioned as the USS *Langley* in March 1922. The Japanese commissioned their first aircraft carrier that December, the *Hosho*, a relatively small ship of only 7,470 tons displacement, but capable of storing and operating up to twenty-six aircraft. This remarkable achievement was all the more impressive for her pioneering installation of an experimental light and mirror landing approach system. An historical irony about *Hosho* is that, of the ten aircraft carriers with which the Imperial Japanese fought the Second World War, only *Hosho* survived that conflict.

In the course of these developments, there were a number of incidents—teething pains—that had to be endured for progress to be achieved. One such involved the Royal Navy pilot, Squadron-Commander E.H. Dunning who was serving aboard HMS *Furious* in the summer of 1917. *Furious* was quite fast for her time, and Dunning believed that the speed of the ship would be a primary factor in the development of a routinely safe landing procedure for his pilots. His squadron was flying the agile Sopwith Pup biplane which Dunning thought of as "easily and gently coaxed over the flight deck of the ship to a safe and acceptable landing." *Furious* was not equipped with arrestor wires, but Dunning decided to have rope handles fitted to his aircraft. He told the deck hands to grip the handles once he had landed, and hold the little Pup firmly on the flight deck. On 2 August 1917, he approached *Furious* and made the first successful carrier deck landing on a ship that was steaming into the wind. But, in another landing attempt two days later, one of the tyres of his aircraft burst as he touched down on the deck. The Sopwith cartwheeled and plummeted off the edge into the sea before the deck

hands could restrain it. Dunning drowned in the accident, but it was a factor in leading to the Royal Navy accepting that a much larger hull was needed to provide a far greater deck area, one similar in size to that of a conventional airfield. The safety of its pilots and aircrew required such a change.

The problem of how to plan this new kind of warship, of how to break up its useful space and position its essential structures, the bridge and funnel and flight deck, to best effect, was one that challenged the greatest of the naval architects. They would ultimately agree the best solution required a full-length flight deck that was virtually free of any obstructions to the safety of aircraft launch and recovery operations. They had to begin with the premise that, for the sake of the most achievable safety and practicality, take-offs must be made from the forward end of the ship and landings must be made on the aft end. A major consideration, of course, was where to put the massive funnel in order to somehow minimize the visibility hazard to the approaching and landing aviators posed by the smoke of the ship's boiler gases. Various ideas were proposed across the years of carrier development. A ducting system was considered in which the smoke discharge was carried by an array of ducting, towards the stern of the ship rather than allowing it to eminate from amidships. But the problem created by smoke from the funnel flowing across the flight deck was never adequately resolved until the coming of nuclear power for the aircraft carrier and smokeless power in the 1960s. The eventual ultimate carrier layout in the interim had the island superstructure positioned to the starboard side of the flight deck, with the navigation platform high in the structure and the funnel behind it. This was relatively efficient, if not always to the advantage of landing aviators.

Another vital design consideration was that of the transverse arrestor wire landing system, the technique for which having been tested and perfected aboard the U.S. Navy carriers *Saratoga* and the

top left The Fairey Albacore was a torpedo-reconnaissance biplane developed from the Swordfish torpedo bomber; top right: SBD dive-bomber of the carrier *Lexington*; above: TBD-1 Devastators of the USS *Saratoga*; left: HMS *Ocean* was commissioned in 1945 and served in the Korean War in 1951.

Lexington in 1927. It was thought that the then-high speed of these ships—thirty-four knots—would mean fulfillment of the prophecy of the early French aviator Clement Ader. In 1891, more than twelve years before that first flight of the Wright brothers, Ader had been asked by the French Minister of War to design, build and test a new two-seat aircraft to carry a light bombload for the military. He did the work, flew and crashed the craft at Satorg on 14 October 1891, losing a handsome potential contract with the government for the warplane. But Ader was nothing if not an aviation visionary with a unique and imaginative view of the future. He believed, for example, that current concepts of land warfare would be wholly transformed through the use of aerial reconnaissance, as would the warfare of fleets at sea. He originated the term porte-avions (aircraft carrier), writing that such specially-designed and developed ships would one day transport their aircraft to sea and would be unlike any other vessels, with clear and unimpeded flight decks. "An aeroplane-carrying vessel is indispensable. These vessels will be constructed on a plan very different from what is currently used. First of all the deck will be cleared of all obstacles. It will be flat, as wide as possible without jeopardizing the nautical lines of the hull, and it will look like a landing field." He predicted that they would have elevators to take the aircraft (with their wings folded) from the flight deck to stowage below for repairs and servicing and bring them back up again, and that the carriers would operate at a high rate of speed. Ader's predictions largely came to fruition in the 1930s, even within the restrictive climate of severe economic depression. It still proved to be a time of substantial progress in the development of carriers, their aircraft and tactics.

In those days the British government was forced by the looming threat of German post-World War One rearmament to reconsider the needs of Britain's own armed forces. To this point the management (frequently mismanagement) of the British Fleet Air Arm had been under the control of the Air Ministry. The state of its aircraft was clearly less than state-of-the-art and the service had, since the formation of the new Royal Air Force in 1918, lost many of its best Royal Naval Air Service pilots through absorption into the RAF. By 1937, the growing inter-service rivalry led to the government reassigning responsibility for British naval aviation to the Royal Navy.

The agenda of Britain and the United States in the Washington Naval Treaty Conference of 1922 included a redefinition of the naval power of the signatories. It further included a blatant determination to minimize battleship construction and set about the imposition of rationing heavy warship construction. That determination of the principal nations was ultimately implemented, not as a result of the treaty participants adhering to the type and tonnage limitations they had imposed on themselves, but largely due to a treaty clause they had also included. They allowed themselves the option to convert any unfinished battleship hulls for completion as aircraft carriers.

The conference applied strict limits on battleship and battlecruiser tonnages for the main navies following the First World War, along with limits of both the total of aircraft carrier tonnage allowed each navy and an upper limit (27,000 tons) for each carrier. According to the rules of the conference, actual fleet units were counted, while experimental vessels were not, and the total tonnage allowed could not be exceeded. All the major navies, though, did exceed the tonnage allowances for their battleships, while all were substantially under-tonnage on their aircraft carriers, which resulted in their converting many battleships and battlecruisers then in service or under construction into aircraft carriers.

Britain's decision to complete her unfinished battleships *Rodney* and *Nelson*, as battleships would

A Boeing F3B1 carrier-based fighter-bomber taking off from the flight deck of the USS *Lexington* in 1929.

later be seen as a mistake when they proved incapable of more than a twenty-three knot top speed when the newest aircraft carriers had top speeds in excess of thirty knots. The navies of Japan and the United States, however, opted for the carrier choice and so were able to launch their new fast carriers in the same year as *Nelson* and *Rodney* were launched. By this time, the aeroplanes being designed and coming on stream for carrier-borne operation were mostly larger, heavier, and faster, requiring ever more flight deck length for their take-offs and landings, and certainly more stowage space. The British, though, had elected to convert the *Furious* to a proper aircraft carrier but in doing so they mistakenly decided to combine a flush flight deck with a short bow flying-off deck, undoubtedly for both utility and economy. They repeated that error in the designs of both *Glorious* and *Courageous,* sister ships of *Furious*. Very soon the bow flying-off decks became obsolete, leaving the British, who had for so long paved the way in aircraft carrier design and innovation, trailing in the wake of others, especially that of the Americans.

The first full-length flat-deck carrier was HMS *Argus*, a British conversion completed in September 1918. She was followed a few years later by the American USS *Langley*, an experimental conversion which, as such, did not count under treaty terms against America's aircraft carrier tonnage limitation.

The 1924 HMS *Hermes* was actually designed ahead of Japan's carrier *Hosho* and her layout and features influenced the design of the Japanese vessel. *Hosho* was completed and commissioned before *Hermes*, however, her commissioning having been delayed by testing, experimentation and budgetary problems. When completed, *Hermes* was the first aircraft carrier to have the classic look, features, and layout of the majority of aircraft carriers to be built in future years. Her sister ship, HMS *Eagle*, also featured a full-length flight deck and a starboard-side island control tower. Unlike *Hermes,* however, *Eagle* was not a purpose-built carrier, but a converted battleship and her final design was less integrated than that of the *Hermes*. *Hermes* featured a new "hurricane bow", sealed up to the flight deck, a feature also found on the new US Navy *Lexington* class carriers, along with substantial anti-aircraft gun batteries.

The history of the aircraft carrier actually began with balloon carriers. In July 1849 when *Vulcano*, a ship of the Austrian Navy, was used for the launching a several small Montgolfiere hot air balloons for the purpose of dropping bombs on Venice. Thwarted by high winds, the attempt mainly failed when most of the balloons were driven back over the ship. One of the bombs, however, did fall on the city. The next event of significance involving balloons in a military context occurred during the American Civil War, when a coal barge, the *George Washington Parke Custis*, was employed as a launching platform and Professor Thaddeus Lowe, Chief Aeronaut of the Union Army Balloon Corps, made reconnaissance ascents over the Potomac River in what he then proclaimed were the first successful "aerial ventures ever from a water-borne vessel". Later, in the First World War, the use of balloons was extended with the advent of balloon carriers or tenders employed by the navies of Britain, France, Russia, Germany, Italy and Sweden. By the end of the war the tenders had mostly been converted to seaplane tenders. This then led to the development of the first ship designed to be an aircraft carrier, exemplified by the French vessel *Le Canard* and inspired by the first seaplane, invented in the spring of 1910. The first seaplane carrier, commissioned in December 1911, was the French *La Foudre*, a tender which carried her seaplanes under hangars on the main deck, from which they were lowered by crane onto the sea. She was later modified with the addition of a ten-metre flat deck for the launching of her aircraft.

In 1913, the British converted HMS *Hermes* into an experimental seaplane carrier, the first in the Royal Navy. She would later be converted to a cruiser, and then back again to a seaplane carrier in 1914, and in October of that year she was sunk by a German submarine. The first American seaplane tender was the USS *Mississippi* late in 1913.

A first in a combat role was achieved in September 1914 when, in the Battle of Tsingtao, the *Wakamiya*, a seaplane carrier of the Imperial Japanese Navy, mounted the world's first successful naval-launched air raids. Four Maurice Farman seaplanes were lowered from the deck of the *Wakamiya* and took off to bombard German forces, after which they returned and were hauled aboard the mother ship. And on Christmas Day, 1914, twelve seaplanes from the British cross-Channel steamers HMS *Riviera, Empress,* and *Engadine,* which had been converted into seaplane carriers, attacked the Zeppelin base at Cuxhaven and damaged a German warship, in an early demonstration of attack by ship-borne aircraft. Examples of the successful use of catapult-launched seaplanes from warships up to and through the Second World War include the float-equipped Fairey Swordfish of the battleship HMS *Warspite* which, in the Second Battle of Narvik in 1940, spotted for the guns of the British warships and participated in the sinking of seven German destroyers and the German submarine *U-64.*

As the role of the aircraft carrier evolved and developed through the 1930s, three basic types of aircraft were found to meet the primary requirements of the major navies: torpedo bombers which were also employed in conventional bombing and reconnaissance roles; dive-bombers, which also doubled in the reconnaissance task; and fighters for bomber escort and fleet defence. The space limitations of the carriers meant that the designs of all these aircraft, were relatively small overall size, with single-engine power, and folding wings. A further development of the period was the armoured flight deck, effectively protecting the hangar deck below.

In the mid-1930s, U.S. President Franklin Roosevelt proposed the conversion of a number of *Cleveland* class cruisers whose keels and hulls were already laid down, to be what would become known as escort carriers or CVLs in the U.S. Navy. They were to be light and small, which were to be utilitarian but not particularly fast and not intended to keep up with the fast fleet carriers like *Lexington* and *Saratoga.* One example of the Royal Navy's version of such a vessel was HMS *Hermes* of 1959, a vessel which would serve in 1982 as the flagship of British forces in the Falklands War. As of 2013, *Hermes* was still serving . . . in the Indian Navy as INS *Viraat.*

As the Second World War began, Britain desperately needed the food, fuel, weapons, ammunition, supplies and other aid that could only be provided by Atlantic merchant shipping convoys from North America. To help protect these convoys, the British designed and developed Merchant Aircraft Carriers, vessels that had flat decks and accommodated six aircraft. A maintenance capability for the aircraft was limited and there was no hangar facility, but these interim vessels served as some protection until the arrival of the CVEs, dedicated escort aircraft carriers built in the United States. The CVEs were only about one-third the size of the fast fleet carriers and operated a small air wing of about twenty to thirty anti-submarine aircraft. They came to be through the use of two basic hull designs: one from a merchant ship, the other from a tanker, the latter being a bit larger and faster. In addition to their duties in the defence of the convoys, the CVEs were heavily employed in transporting military aircraft to various war theaters. Some also took part in campaigns such as the Battle of Samar in the liberation of the Philippines, where six of the escort carriers and their own destroyer escorts attacked five Japanese battleships, forcing them to retreat.

Another interesting British idea put into use in the interim between the period of the Merchant Aircraft Carriers and the escort carriers was the CAM ship or Catapult Aircraft Merchantman. This was a merchant vessel equipped with a catapult and a war-weary Hawker Hurricane fighter from which it was launched for convoy protection duties. With its mission completed, the Hurricane could

below: Women in naval aviation at NAS Pensacola in 1918.

below: U.S. Navy float planes lined up at NAS Pensacola in the early 1930s.

not land back aboard the CAM ship and, unless it was within range of land would have to ditch in the sea. The CAM ships and aircraft operated for more than two years and relatively few launches were made in all that time, but their record included the downing of six enemy bombers for the loss of just one British pilot.

One of the handful of RAF pilots who flew the dangerous and demanding "Hurricat" missions, as the aircraft were known, was Dicky Turley-George, a Hurricane pilot who was stationed at RAF Tangmere on the Sussex coast in the Battle of Britain. At Tangmere, Dicky met Ann, who would become his wife. Ann: "I was Hitler's secret weapon. I was a cook and served in the Officer's Mess." Dicky survived the Battle of Britain and volunteered to serve with the Merchant Ships Fighter Unit which was based at Speke Airfield, near Liverpool. With high revs and rocket-boosted power, he was launched from the merchant vessels, and usually finished up in the sea. He was involved in the downing of German Condor multi-engined maritime aircraft: "Being launched was easy. You were strapped in tightly, kept your elbows tucked into your hips, then, as the ship breasted a wave you pressed the fire button and, with quite a lot of power on, you climbed away."

The aircraft carrier really came into its own in the Second World War, taking on a substantial part of the action in the major theaters and campaigns. It was then that she inherited the mantle of capital ship of the great navies by virtue of her mobility and the enormous and highly effective strength of her air wing. The battleship had done impressive service throughout most of the two previous centuries, but the ability of the aircraft carrier to project national power, to reach and strike the enemy anywhere guaranteed her succession and leadership role in naval warfare. With the advent of the nuclear-powered supercarrier in the 1960s, and her accompanying battle and strike group of escorting warships and submarines, that leadership role was clearly established for the foreseeable future.

In the early part of the Second World War, however, aircraft carriers sometimes went into battle with a greater vulnerability than that of their predecessors, the traditional battleships. While the navies of Germany and Italy in that time possessed no carriers of their own, they more than held their own in situations where enemy carriers were forced into gun-range encounters. The first example of an aircraft carrier to be lost in the war was that of HMS *Courageous*, originally built as a cruiser but rebuilt as a carrier, which was sunk by the German submarine *U-29* on 17 September 1939. That was followed in the Norwegian campaign of 1940 when HMS *Glorious* was sunk by the German battlecruisers *Scharnhorst* and *Gneisenau*, 8 June 1940.

The carrier soon established her strength and versatility though, when in November 1940, the Royal Navy's HMS *Illustrious* launched a long-range raid by twenty-one Swordfish torpedo bombers on warships of the Italian fleet in the harbour at Taranto, the first such strike to be so effectively planned and successfully executed. Lieutenant Commander John Wellham, Fleet Air Arm, flew one of the Swordfish aircraft [called Stringbag by some] in that raid: "I was serving in HMS *Eagle*, a very old carrier which had been in the fleet for some years. We came to the Mediterranean at a time when it was obvious that Mussolini was going to come into the war on the side of the Germans. He'd been sitting on the sidelines, waiting to see which side was likely to produce the most glory for him. As the Germans were sweeping through Europe, it was clearly going to be their side that he wanted to join. We, therefore, were sent to join the Mediterranean fleet, which we did but a few weeks before Mussolini came into the war.

"Led by Sir Andrew Cunningham, a wildly enthusiastic chap, we tore around the Med looking for someone with whom to be hostile, and actually only found the Italian fleet at sea once. We attacked them twice in four hours with our Swordfish torpedo bombers. Unfortunately, there were only nine of us making the attacks, quite inadequate against a fast-moving fleet. So it was necessary for us to catch them in harbour. Our admiral did his homework and found that attacking enemy ships in harbour had been quite successful right back to 300 bc.

"The RAF had a squadron of Bristol Blenheims in the area, which they were using for reconnaissance of the various North African harbours, including Bomba. One day they told us about a submarine depot ship at Bomba with a submarine alongside it. They did a recce for us the next morning and discovered another submarine coming into the harbour, so the three of us went off in our Swordfish and, at Bomba, spotted the large submarine on the surface, obviously recharging its batteries. Our leader put his torpedo into it and the sub blew up and sank very satisfactorily. The other chap and I went on and as we got closer we found that, not only was there a depot ship and a submarine, there was a destroyer between the two of them. I let my torpedo go towards the depot ship. My colleague dropped his from the other side and it went underneath the submarine and hit the destroyer. I was very excited and was shouting. Things were going up in the air and we discovered that all four ships had sunk, which was confirmed later by aerial reconnaissance. That night the Italians admitted on the radio that they had lost four ships in the harbour. However, they said that the loss was due to an

below: A Fairey Swordfish is readied for flight aboard an escort carrier of the Royal Navy in the Second World War; right: The Italian battleship *Conti de Cavour* the day after the Royal Navy attack on the Italian fleet at Taranto, November 1940.

overwhelming force of motor torpedo boats and torpedo bombers which had attacked them during the night. If I had been commanding officer of that base, I would have reported something along those same lines. I certainly wouldn't have been prepared to admit that three elderly biplanes had sunk four of my ships.

"The attack on the ships in harbour at Bomba had confirmed for us, and for Cunningham, that the best way to attack ships was when they were in harbour. He then decided that an attack on the main Italian fleet in their base at Taranto was imperative. That was all very well, but we in *Eagle* had a limited number of aircraft and no long-range fuel tanks to get us there and back. We also needed absolutely up-to-date reconnaissance to do an attack like that. Then the new carrier *Illustrious* came to join us, bringing us the long-range tanks we needed. The Royal Air Force provided a flight of three Martin Maryland bombers for the reconnaissance work, and they were very good for that. They had the speed, the training and the ability, and each day at dawn and dusk they gave us reports on the positions of ships in Taranto. We couldn't have done the job without them. "The go-ahead was given for the raid because both *Illustrious* and *Eagle* were fully prepared to do it—but then complications arose. *Illustrious* had a fire in the hangar deck which caused a delay. Meanwhile, *Eagle*, which had been bombed

repeatedly by the aircraft of the Reggia Aeronautica, had developed plumbing problems. When we tried to fuel our aircraft we weren't quite sure what we were fueling them with, and so *Eagle* was scrubbed from the operation. We went on with the plan, however, and transferred five aircraft and eight crews over to *Illustrious*.

"The attack was called Operation Judgement and it was set for 11 November 1940. Diversionary actions involving merchant navy convoys elsewhere in the Med were organized and worked well, disguising the fact that we were going to hit Taranto.

"We went off in two waves, some of us with bombs, some with torpedoes. The Martin recce flights had shown us that the Italian battleships were in the Mar Grande, the largest part of Taranto harbour, while destroyers, cruisers, submarines and various auxiliary vessels were in the inner harbour, Mar Piccolo.

"At Taranto, I had to dodge a barrage balloon and in doing so I was hit by flak which broke the aileron control spar, and I couldn't move the control column, which is very embarrassing in the middle of a dive. So, using brute force and ignorance, I cleared the column enough to get it fully over to the right. While this was going on and I was trying to get the thing to fly properly, I suddenly appreciated that I was diving right into the middle of Taranto City, which was obviously not a good thing. So I hauled the plane out of the dive, found the target and attacked it. But when you drop 2,000 pounds off an aircraft of that weight, it rises. There is nothing you can do about it, and it rose into the flak from the battleship I was attacking. I was hit again and got a hole about a metre long by at least a half-metre wide. The Swordfish still flew and we got back 200 miles over the sea with the aircraft in that condi-

When the British Fleet Air Arm attacked the warships of the Italian fleet in Taranto harbour on 11/12 November 1940, John Wellham, left, piloted one of the Swordfish biplanes in the raid; above: The crew of another of the Fairey torpedo bombers with their aircraft. The successful attack later had a powerful influence on the Japanese admirals who planned the surprise attack on American battleships and port facilities in Pearl Harbor, Hawaii, on 7 December 1941; right: John Wellham aboard HMS *Illustrious* in 1999.

tion. It was very painful because, to fly straight, I had to keep left rudder on all the time, which is bad for your ankle, but we got home."

Commander Charles Lamb, RN, from his book *War in a Stringbag*: "When a carrier turns into wind to receive her aircraft, it seems to be lazy, leisurely movement to the approaching pilot, about to land. The bow starts to turn, imperceptibly to begin with, and then more emphatically in a graceful sweeping arc. The stern seems to kick the other way, as though resisting the motion, and then gives way in a rush, causing a mighty wash astern. While the ship is turning, the wind across the flight-deck can be violently antagonistic to a pilot who tries to land before the turn has been completed. Since we were about to run out of petrol, the turn seemed interminable, and after one-half circuit of the ship I decided to risk the cross-wind, and the violent turning motion and get down before it was too late."

Bill Sarra and his observer, Jack Bowker, were flying in the diversionary bombing element of the first strike of Swordfish on the harbour at Taranto. They had been briefed to drop their bombs on the cruisers, destroyers, or oil storage tanks in the inner harbour, the Mar Piccolo. Sarra was unable to discern the specified targets and crossed over the dockyard. It was then that he spotted the hangars of the Italian seaplane base just ahead. He released his bombs from an altitude of 500 feet and watched as one made a direct hit on a hangar, with the others blasting the slipways. The anti-aircraft fire was intense, but Sarra and Bowker returned safely to the carrier *Illustrious*. The Royal Navy victory at Taranto that night meant that the balance of capital ship power in the Mediterranean had been shifted in favour of the Allies. The first awards made to participants in the Taranto strike were few indeed. Six months later in a supplementary list, Sarra and Bowker were 'mentioned in despatches', but by then they were both prisoners of war.

"You were throwing the aircraft about like a madman, half the time, and every time I tried to look over the side, the slipstream nearly ripped off my goggles! The harbour was blanked out by ack-ack and I had to check with the compass to see which way we were facing!" —from *War in a Stringbag* by Charles Lamb, RN

When the United States entered the Second World War she had only three aircraft carriers operating in the Pacific, and only seven carriers in total. Japan began the war with the largest, most modern carrier fleet in the world, ten great warships. She would lose nine of them in the conflict. Influenced heavily by the success of the British raid on the Italian fleet at Taranto late in 1940, the Japanese prepared to attack American battleships and installations in Pearl Harbor, Hawaii. Their attack would come on 7 December 1941 and would involve the use of specially modified aerial torpedoes for use in shallow water. The attack would profoundly demonstrate the powerful capability of a large force of modern aircraft carriers. No such carrier force had ever been unleashed against another nation in naval history.

The army, naval and air forces of Japan then began a seemingly relentless campaign across the western Pacific and throughout Southeast Asia. North of Singapore, off the east coast of Malaya, they attacked and sank the British battleship *Prince of Wales* and the battlecruiser *Repulse*, with land-based bombers and torpedo bombers of the Imperial Japanese Navy. It was history's first example of aircraft sinking a battleship which was fighting and manoeuvring at sea.

In April 1942, in reprisal for the Japanese surprise attack on the United States at Pearl Harbor, a bombing raid by sixteen U.S. Army Air Corps B-25 Mitchell bombers was staged and led by Lt Col.

Jimmy Doolittle. The bombers were transported aboard the carrier USS *Hornet* (CV-8) to a point from which they were launched to fly the attack on targets in Tokyo, a relatively token strike, but one that shocked the Japanese people who had been led to believe that they were quite safe from enemy attack on their home islands.

More significant carrier actions would follow, including the historic Battle of Midway, probably the most important battle of the Pacific campaign in the war. It took place between 4 and 7 June 1942, six months after the Pearl Harbor attack. In it the carrier-based aircraft of the U.S. Navy stunningly and decisively defeated the Imperial Japanese Navy, sinking four of the six IJN carriers present, a blow from which the Japanese would not recover . . . the worst Japanese naval defeat in 350 years. In the Midway action, the Japanese Navy had planned to lure the American carriers into a trap as a part of their intention to occupy Midway Island in a response to the Doolittle raid on Tokyo. But the Americans had been forewarned of the Japanese plan when U.S. codebreakers learned the date, location and details of the enemy plan, enabling the American Navy to plan an ambush of its own.

Following the Midway operation, the U.S. island-hopping campaign in the western Pacific, its attrition, and the gathering strength of America's military industrial output, coupled with Japan's inability to keep pace in replacing her losses in ships and pilots, dictated her decline in the conflict. Her once-powerful carrier-led striking force would never again threaten the Allies in the Pacific Theater of Operations.

right: Japanese Admiral Isoroku Yamamoto, a Harvard-educated former Naval Attaché in Washington, and the leading planner of the air strike at Pearl Harbor on 7 December of 1941, which drew the United States into the Second World War; below: A woman war worker at the Grumman aircraft plant in 1943.

By the autumn of 1940 the United States had grown intolerant of the aggressive expansionist policy of the Japanese Empire of the late 1930s. Japanese armed forces had moved into Manchuria and then onto mainland China as part of a plan they referred to as the Great East Asia Co-Prosperity Sphere. Fed up with this behaviour and Japan's military incursions, the American government acted to impose an embargo on Japan covering all war-related materials including steel, scrap iron, and aviation spirit. Additionally, all Japanese assets in the United States were frozen.

In the pursuit of their plans, Japanese military officials were deeply concerned about the shortages of strategic commodities they faced. With limited natural resources they determined that, in order to succeed in China they would have to gain access to tin, rubber, bauxite and especially, oil, from the Dutch East Indies and Malaya. To do so required them to go to war with both the British Empire and the Dutch government in exile. They believed, too, that they would almost certainly be compelled to fight the Americans, who had a military presence in the Philippines and the Pacific and would not tolerate such an action by the Japanese. In anticipation of such a conflict with the U.S., the Japanese military planners formulated a series of attacks they would carry out on American bomber bases in the Philippines, and on the U.S. Pacific Fleet warships and facilities at Pearl Harbor, Hawaii. They were convinced that these particular targets would have to be hit hard and destroyed to pave the way for their forces to take the East Indies, Malaya, and China.

The man the Japanese chose to conceive, plan and direct a breathtaking surprise attack on Pearl Harbor was Harvard-educated Admiral Isoroku Yamamoto. Having once served in Washington as a naval attaché, this brilliant tactician had no illusions about the military strength and capability of the United States or her quality as an adversary. He did not favour war with her, but had accepted its inevitability and he warned his colleagues that in such a war, it would be absolutely essential to "give a fatal blow to the enemy at the outset, when it was least expected." Anything less than the total destruction of the American fleet would, in his opinion, "awaken a sleeping giant."

Yamamoto had been fascinated by the theories of a British naval authority, Hector Bywater, whose 1921 book, *Sea Power in the Pacific*, had been widely read in Japan and become required reading at the Imperial Naval Academy and the Japanese Naval War College by the following year. Bywater believed that the Japanese home islands were fundamentally protected from direct assault by U.S. forces because of the distance and the secondary supply and fuel consumption involved in such an effort. He proposed that, in a Pacific war, American success against Japan would be linked to a U.S. island-hopping campaign through the Marianas, to Guam and the Philippines. He followed his first book with another in 1925, *The Great Pacific War*, in which his premise was that Japan's empire could become invulnerable if she launched a successful surprise attack on the U.S. Pacific fleet, invaded Guam and the Philippines, and fortified her mandate islands.

Admiral Yamamoto went to London in 1934 and invited Bywater to meet with him in his suite at Grosvenor House to discuss the author's theories and their implications for the stratagies of both Japan and the U.S.

In his planning for the Sunday 7 December 1941 attack on the capital ships of the U.S. Navy at Pearl Harbor, he knew that several key American warships were either undergoing refit on the American west coast where they were stationed, or were in transit between the west coast and Hawaii. He knew that it would probably not be possible, therefore, to destroy the entire American Pacific fleet in a single strike, and he devised a master plan that included an essential second strike on what remained of that fleet, to be carried out six months after the attack on Pearl. He knew too, that the

above: Aircraft of the Imperial Japanese Navy are made ready to take off in the 1941 surprise attack on the American warships at anchor in Pearl Harbor, Hawaii; far right: The ruin of the USS *Oklahoma* after the raid on the U.S. battleships in the naval basin facility at Pearl.

left: The battleship USS *West Virginia* burning furiously at her anchorage in Pearl Harbor after being attacked by naval aircraft of Japan on 7 December 1941. The next afternoon U.S. President Franklin D. Roosevelt asked the Congress to declare war on Japan, followed by war declarations on Germany and Italy, Japan's Axis allies in the Second World War; At bottom: An example of a patriotic matchbook produced after the Pearl Harbor raid.

Strike 'em Dead

REMEMBER PEARL HARBOR

CLOSE COVER BEFORE STRIKING

U.S. Pacific fleet included just three aircraft carriers, the *Lexington* and *Enterprise*, and the *Saratoga*, which was then in port on the U.S. west coast. He was comforted by that knowledge, in view of his being able to field six carriers for the Pearl Harbor attack.

Historians have often disagreed over the degree to which Yamamoto and the Japanese military planners had been influenced by the techniques and results of the British air attack on the Italian fleet warships at Taranto in November 1940, in the planning of the Pearl Harbor raid. It seems clear, however, that they were certainly interested in the Taranto air strike by Swordfish torpedo bombers flying from HMS *Illustrious* to inflict major damage on the Italian fleet, putting half of it out of action. They were intrigued that the Fleet Air Arm of the Royal Navy had obviously solved the problem of how to deliver torpedoes against warship targets anchored in a shallow harbour.

There were similarities between Pearl Harbor and Taranto. Both were considered safe and proper anchorages by their fleet occupants; both were well defended and seen as significant threats to any adversary; and both were adjacent to cities with populations of about 200,000. The American naval facility at Pearl clearly threatened Japan's intentions for Southeast Asia, and the Italian fleet in Taranto threatened the sea lanes between Britain and her interests in Gibraltar, Egypt, India and Singapore.

Both the British planners of the Taranto raid and the Japanese who planned the attack on Pearl had to cope with and overcome substantial barriers to their success. The crews of the carrier-based Swordfish aircraft attacking Taranto had to make their run at the port from the Mediterranean, avoiding discovery by Italian reconnaissance aircraft, evading the attentions of more than fifty enemy warships and more than twenty anti-aircraft shore batteries. They had to avoid the steel cables of roughly fifty barrage balloons, as well as many squadrons of Italian fighter planes. To succeed in their attack on the U.S. fleet at Pearl, Yamamoto and the Japanese had to stage an effective surprise attack after first assembling a powerful thirty-two-warship task force that included six aircraft carriers—*Akagi, Hiryu, Kaga, Shokaku, Soryu,* and *Zuikaku* in the Kurile Islands north of Japan. That force had to steam some 4,000 miles without being detected and without being resupplied, to a point within 200 miles of Oahu, Hawaii. After doing so, the carrier-based Imperial Japanese Navy aircraft had to approach and evade the defensive fire of many shore batteries, that of up to sixty-eight warships and more than 100 American fighter planes.

Physically, Pearl Harbor is a shallow basin that surrounds an airfield facility called Ford Island. The harbour is connected to the sea by a single narrow channel and adjoins the site of the present-day Honolulu airport. A large oil storage tank farm, drydocks and a submarine base occupy the eastern edge of the harbour. On 7 December 1941, the day of the Japanese attack, seven battleships of the U.S. Pacific fleet were anchored southeast of Ford Island; they were the *Arizona, California, Maryland, Nevada, Oklahoma, Tennessee,* and *West Virginia.* An eighth battleship, the *Pennsylvania,* was in a nearby drydock.

The most difficult challenge for the Japanese in planning their attack on Pearl was the successful delivery of their torpedoes by aircraft into the shallow basin of the harbour. Contemporary torpedo technology—prior to the Taranto raid—meant that a torpedo would sink to a depth of about seventy feet before levelling and going on to its target. In Pearl's basin, the weapon would simply become mired in the muddy bottom. With the inspiration of the successful British torpedo attack on warships at Taranto, the problem was given to munitions engineers of the Nagasaki-based Mitsubishi Company who worked overtime to develop and perfect a torpedo with a new stabilizing fin. When properly dropped, the new weapon would sink to less than the forty-foot depth of Pearl Harbor before continuing to its target. Before the carriers left Japanese waters for the area near Hawaii, 180 of the new torpedoes were loaded aboard the six Japanese carriers of the Pearl task force.

22 November 1941. Japanese special envoys Saburo Kurusu and Kichisaburo Nomura had been sent to Washington to explore through diplomatic means resolution of differences between the American and Japanese governments. Their efforts were failing as the IJN task force was being assembled. On 25 November the Japanese warships headed east from Hitokappu Bay in the Kuriles for the waters off Hawaii, the six carriers being escorted by battleships, heavy cruisers, destroyers and submarines, all observing strict radio silence in an effort to reach their destination undected.

The commander of the task force, Vice Admiral Chiuchi Nagumo, received a coded signal from Admiral Yamamoto on 2 December: "Nitaka Yama Nabora", Climb Mount Nitaka, which authorized him to begin the attack operation.

The task force arrived at the launch point north of Oahu and by 6 a.m. the first wave of attacking dive-bombers, horizontal bombers, torpedo bombers and fighters was rising from the carrier *Akagi*. The mass of aircraft was led by Lieutenant Commander Mitsuo Fuchida who signalled the carrier force as his planes rounded Barber's Point southwest of Pearl at 7.53 a.m., that they had reached the objective and were beginning the attack.

The U.S. Navy destroyer *Shaw* exploding during the Japanese raid on Pearl Harbor in 1941.

far left: Pearl Harbor prior to the raid of 7 December 1941, with the U.S. battleships at anchor off Ford Island; left: The USS *California* burning at her mooring after being hit in the attack; below: Huge oil fires from some of the battleships struck by Japanese bombs and torpedoes in the attack.

The early morning calm surrounding the battleships at anchor that bright Sunday was shattered as the torpedo bombers descended over the basin towards their targets. The first torpedoes slammed into a light cruiser, a minelayer, and the battleship *Arizona*, ripping out the bottom of her hull. The next to receive torpedoes were the battleships *Oklahoma* and *California*, each struck by three of the missiles, wrecking them. *Oklahoma* was then hit by a fourth torpedo which caused her to capsize. A bomb fell on *Arizona*, exploding in her forward magazine and tearing her apart. Upwards of a thousand of her crew died.

Richard McCutcheon was a powder carman in the number two turret of the battleship *West Virginia*. At just before 8 a.m. dive-bombing and torpedo aircraft of the Imperial Japanese Navy appeared over the American battleships in the harbour. The *West Virginia* was hit and severely damaged in the ensuing attack and her crew was ordered to abandon ship. McCutcheon jumped into the water and swam for the nearby shore. On reaching it he was only a short distance from the home of a woman who had been witnessing the attack. When she saw sailors swimming to the shore from the nearest of the burning battleships, she quickly gathered clothing from her husband's closet and started distributing it to McCutcheon and the other seaman as they made their way to shore. "On December 6th a lot of us were out sunning ourselves on the upper deck, until it got so hot that we had to run down and jump in the showers. A typical Saturday in Pearl. It was good duty. A calm regular day. On Sunday morning we had breakfast. I had the duty. My station was to handle a fire extinguisher. That day a third of the ship's company had liberty on shore. The bugle sounded 'Fire and Rescue' and I ran off to get my white hat from my locker. The Officer of the Deck at this point thought that there had been some kind of strange explosion over by Ten-Ten dock. A torpedo had passed under a ship there and hit a cruiser and they both sank. Then we were ordered to General Quarters. I realized it was the Japs and I started running aft. I went up two decks, heading to the turret. On the way I saw a plane and wondered what he was doing. He turned and went toward the *California* and as he turned, I saw the red ball on the wing. Before I got to the turret there was a tremendous explosion somewhere below us. It was a torpedo. The whole ship was shaking and, by then, the ladder was full. I went around to another ladder and got up to the top deck. From there I went up to the boat deck and under the overhang of the turret to my battle station in the turret. The explosions continued, the ship shook and the blast covers clanged. Then we started listing slowly to port, very slowly, and I was watching that and thinking that we might have to get through that hatch door in the bottom of the turret pretty soon. Meanwhile, the damage control officer managed to counter-flood to keep the ship from capsizing. Eventually, she just settled to the bottom.

"The hatch cover was still open and someone stuck his head up and yelled 'Abandon ship!' We got out and there was no big rush. The *Tennessee* was inboard of us and we made it to the fo'c'sle, took our shoes off and jumped into the water. We swam to Ford Island and when we got to shore the first thing we heard was 'Get down, get down. Strafing!' I got down by a truck at the edge of the golf course as a plane turned toward us and began firing. The tracers seemed to be coming right at me. Only one of his guns was firing. I got under the truck and the tracers turned away from me. About then a woman came down from one of the houses there, carrying clothes. I wandered over to see what was going on and she fitted us out with dry clothing."

"High-altitude bombers overhead! a lookout with binoculars reported. I squinted up. Heavy smoke from dozens of fires was darkening the sky. Above it, patches of blue showed amid the drifting cumulus. The planes were at about 10,000 feet and looking smaller than birds. They were flying over the battle line in a single long column from the seaward side. At last, several of our five-inch anti-aircraft guns had ammunition. It had been passed up by hand from the magazines at great sacrifice, I later learned. They opened fire with an ear-piercing crack. The sky was dotted with black puffs of exploding shells from the *California* and many other ships. Bombs began to fall, metallic specks that reflected the sunlight as they wobbled down. The specks grew larger and more ominous. I felt totally helpless. These might well be my last seconds of life. Whether they were or not depended on the skills of an enemy pilot and bombardier, not on anything I could do.

"Properly buttoned-up, the *California* could have shrugged off two or even three torpedoes with minor listing that could have been corrected by counter-flooding the starboard voids. Instead, she had assumed a port list of about fifteen degrees and the list was still increasing. Suddenly I was sliding toward the low side of the birdbath, which brought me up sharply against the splinter shield. My earphones were jerked from my head. Before replacing them I looked down. A hundred feet below me was nothing but dirty, oil-streaked and flotsam-filled water. Lifeless bodies from the *Oklahoma* floated face down. Motor launches were criss-crossing the channel, picking up swimming sailors.

"If the *California* capsized, and that I could see was a distinct possibility, I had at least a fighting chance to join the swimmers. My shipmates below decks had none. I planned to climb to the opposite side of the splinter shield as the ship went over, and launch myself in a long, flat dive when the maintop touched the water. If I could avoid getting fouled in the yardarm rigging or the radio antennas, I just might get clear.

"Ahead of the *Nevada*, a large pipeline snaked out from Ford Island in a semi-circle ending at the dredge *Turbine*. Since it blocked more than half the channel, the line was always disconnected and pulled clear when the battleships were scheduled to stand out. This morning, of course, it was still in place. But the sailor conning the *Nevada* squeezed her between the dredge and the drydock area without slowing down.

"The flames were now shooting up past her anti-aircraft directors nearly to her foretop. She had been hit repeatedly, and Pearl Harbor was pouring into her hull; her bow was low in the water. If she were to sink in the channel, she would plug up the entire harbour like a cork in a bottle. With bitter regret, we watched her run her bow into shallow water between the floating drydock and Hospital Point. The current carried her stern around, and she finished her evolution pointing back up the channel she had tried so valiantly to follow to freedom."—Ted Mason, USS *California*

At the height of his business career Kazuo Sakamaki became the head of Toyota's Brazilian operations. In December 1941, Sakamaki was a twenty-three-year-old ensign in the Imperial Japanese Navy and one-half of the crew of a midget submarine struggling to enter Pearl Harbor. His mission was to sneak into the harbour, unobserved, ahead of the main attack by the aircraft of the IJN, and be ready to sink one of the target battleships at the appropriate moment. It was a suicide mission involving five such midget subs. But the gyro-compass of Sakamaki's boat failed and the other four subs were either lost or destroyed during the attack. Sakamaki's boat became stranded on a coral reef down the coast and he was forced to abandon it. He was later discovered, unconscious, by an American soldier and became the first Japanese prisoner of war in World War Two. He recalled feeling deep shame with the failure of his mission, for letting his sub fall into enemy hands, and for surviving when his comrades had all died in the attempted raid. In time though, he gradually overcame the guilt he felt and went on to help his fellow Japanese prisoners in POW camps in the United States.

In the aftermath of the Japanese raid on the American ships and facilities at Pearl Harbor, Hawaii, on 7 December 1941, it became clear that the results might have been far more favourable for the Japanese had they been more efficient in the effort.

Certain of the key targets at Pearl, the U.S. machine shops and the large oil storage tank farm were mainly unaffected by the attack, and most significantly, the Japanese had failed to block the narrow and shallow single entrance to the harbour. Had they been able to sink a ship in that tiny channel, they would have denied the U.S. Navy access to Pearl for some time. In failing to destroy the machine shops, they allowed essential repair work to begin immediately on the U.S. warships heavily damaged in the raid. The U.S. ships in Pearl that were still seaworthy, and those that had avoided the attack through being elsewhere, were left able to function and fight owing to the fuel available from the intact tank farm. In time, nearly eighty per cent of the U.S. aircraft that had been damaged seemingly beyond repair, at Pearl and other American airfields in Hawaii, were repaired and made fully operational again.

The U.S. Navy battleships *West Virginia* and *Tennessee* ablaze in the Pearl Harbor raid.

Escort Service

The escort aircraft carrier, known in U.S. Navy circles as a "jeep carrier" or "baby flattop" was a relatively small and somewhat slow vessel employed by the British Royal Navy, the Imperial Japanese Navy and Army Air Force, and the U.S. Navy during the Second World War. Most examples were roughly half the length and a third the displacement of the larger fleet carriers of these services. Of 151 aircraft carriers built in the United States during the Second World War, 122 were escort carriers. Of these, by far the most numerous were the vessels of the *Casablanca* and *Bogue* classes. Slower, with less armour and armament and a smaller complement of aircraft aboard, these ships were also much less expensive to manufacture and could be produced in far less time than the fleet carriers, filling a gap in the active inventory when fleet carriers were still scarce. Their minimal armour and armament, though, made them much more vulnerable to enemy attack and a number of them were sunk with heavy losses.

The limits imposed on the five major naval powers by the Washington Naval Treaty of 1922 defined the maximum size and tonnage of aircraft carriers for their navies. The limits caused insufficient carrier construction in the years between the two world wars. Thus, the operational needs for aircraft carriers could not be met as the Second World War expanded from Europe. The relatively few available fleet aircraft carriers could not possibly cope with the requirements for transporting aircraft to distant bases, supporting amphibious invasions, providing carrier landing training for new pilots, anti-submarine patrols, and providing defensive air cover for deployed battleships and cruisers. Until the availability of more fleet carriers, the navies had to rely on the conversion of existing vessels, and hulls under construction for other purposes, until new purpose-built carriers came on stream.

What followed was the development of a need identified by the U.S. Navy for a type of light aircraft carrier, a CVL, from the conversion of passenger liners and cruisers, into vessels capable of operating at battle fleet speed—these in addition to a classification of warships referred to as escort carriers CVE, naval auxiliary vessels intended for pilot training and for the transport of aircraft to far off bases.

In the 1930s, the Royal Navy needed aircraft carriers to help defend the British trade routes, but little was done about meeting that need until HMS *Audacity* resulted from the conversion of a captured German motor vessel, the MV *Hannover*, which was commissioned in the summer of 1941. Until the later arrival of CVEs from America as part of the Lend-Lease arrangement, Britain had to make do for convoy protection from German aircraft, with fighter-equipped catapult ships and CAM ships equipped with a single, disposable fighter aircraft.

In 1940, the U.S. Chief of Naval Operations authorized the construction of naval auxiliary vessels for aircraft transport, ships that were referred to as auxiliary aircraft escort vessels (AVG), and later as auxiliary aircraft carriers (ACV). These warships first proved their worth in Operation Torch, North Africa, and in the anti-submarine warfare of the Battle of the Atlantic, operating at convoy speeds. By July 1943, these vessels had been upgraded by the U.S. Navy from auxiliary to combatant and had become known as jeep carriers or baby flattops. Their crews soon discovered that the CVEs had a better performance than the light carriers, pitching less in moderate to high seas on their more stable hulls. But their crews also had another reference to the CVEs: combustible, vulnerable, expendable—

Survivors being rescued after the sinking of the U.S. Navy escort carrier *Gambier Bay* during the Battle of Leyte Gulf in October 1944.

left: The USS *Gambier Bay* ferrying aircraft to a Pacific destination in the Second World War; below and bottom: Grumman Wildcats.

owing to their minimal magazine protection in comparison to that of the larger fleet carriers. In Japanese kamikaze suicide plane attacks late in the war, three escort carriers, the USS *St. Lo, Ommaney Bay,* and *Bismarck Sea,* were all destroyed in kamikaze attacks, the largest warships to be sunk in that way.

As the escort carriers were not fast enough to keep pace with task groups of battleships, fleet carriers and cruisers, they were mainly dedicated to the vital role of convoy escort in the Pacific and Atlantic theaters of the war, helping to protect them against the threat of enemy aircraft and submarines. There they also provided vital air support for ground forces during amphibious landing operations. A further important aspect of their participation in the war effort was serving as back-up aircraft transports for the fleet carriers and ferrying aircraft to American and British military units around the world. During the Battle of the Atlantic, the escort carriers were assigned convoy protection duties, dealing with enemy submarine and aircraft attacks initially, and later in the conflict, as part of aggressive hunter-killer groups in search of German U-boats, rather than being formally attached in a convoy escort role.

Out in the Pacific, the escort carriers, under a protective umbrella of the Fast Carrier Task Forces, provided considerable air support to U.S. ground troops in such actions as the Battle of Leyte Gulf.

Some called them "Woolworth Carriers"—the American-built Second World War Lend-Lease escort aircraft carriers of the *Attacker* class which included *Battler, Chaser, Fencer, Hunter, Pursuer, Ravager, Searcher, Stalker, Striker,* and *Tracker*—manufactured by the Ingalls Shipbuilding Corporation of Pascagoula, Mississippi and Western Pipe & Steel, Seattle, Washington, for the British Royal Navy. As part of their convoy escort duties, the small escort carriers provided air scouting, defence against long-range enemy scouting aircraft, and hunting for enemy submarines. These unlovely examples of the aircraft carrier art were certainly not cheap imitations of the real thing. Still, their hardy crews found it necessary to make some adjustments in how they did things aboard these new CVEs. Standard U.S. Navy methods and routine had been built into the design and construction philosophy of these ships in many areas including but not limited to the accommodation for the ship's company, food preparation and service, and in the operational spaces. In comparison with the layouts of most conventional Royal Navy warships of the time, the work spaces were relatively roomy. The "open plan" hangar deck was comparatively spacious relative to that of British-designed fleet carriers which were not as open and airy, or user-friendly. And the hangar facility aboard the new CVEs carried a full-size projection screen that could be lowered to turn the large space into a cinema for the recreation of the crews. The hangar area could also be made cooler and more comfortable in hot weather by lowering the aircraft lift. The aircraft hangar of the CVE normally took up about a third of the length under the flight deck and housed between twenty-four and thirty fighter and bomber aircraft. The hangar space of the larger *Essex* class fleet carrier could house more than 100 fighter, bomber, and torpedo bomber aircraft. And in the construction of British warships of that period, accommodation was made for ratings to sleep in slung hammocks, while in the American-built CVEs, three-level bunks were arranged in units of six which were separated by narrow gangways and positioned in deck spaces well below the hangar deck. When they were not being used, the bunks could be folded up and secured to provide more space. Most CVE crew members, though, thought that the conditions in their living spaces were claustrophobic and unhealthy.

Carrying right on through the supercarriers of today, the bunking areas for the ratings included a small recreational space with chairs and tables for reading, letter writing and card games. Next up the status ladder were the Petty Officers, whose slightly better accommodation afforded them two-berth cabins. They were provided with a relatively spacious wardrobe, a desk, a personal safe and a two-bunk sleeping unit and in some cases, a small amount of additional storage space.

The departments aboard the CVEs included facilities for drying and packing parachutes, metal and wood shops, and a well-equipped sick bay. In the area of food preparation, most dishes were steam-cooked in the galley, unlike the traditional Royal Navy system in which the duty cooks brought food-stuffs from the galley, prepared them on wooden tables and brought them back to the galley for the cooking. On the CVEs, meals were served and eaten cafeteria-style in a central dining room. The ratings ate their meals from from sectioned metal trays, American style. The Petty Officers had their own mess; the officers dined in their own wardroom. Additionally, there was a NAAFI canteen and soda fountain for the men of the British CVEs. The CVEs also operated a laundry and a barber shop. Unlike the escort carriers built for the U.S. Navy, however, modifications made for those of the Royal Navy included a nod for the traditions of that old service. Ice cream making machines were removed; viewed as unnecessary luxuries on these warships which, after all, served grog and other alcoholic beverages. The American heavy duty washing machines of the laundry room were also removed, on the basis that "all a British sailor needs to keep clean is a bucket and a bar of soap."

These Attacker class escort carrier CVEs were relatively simple and utilitarian warships made mainly of prefabricated, welded construction and powered by single-shaft geared turbines capable of driving them through the water at a maximum speed of seventeen knots. They were 492 feet long, with a beam of sixty-nine feet, only a bit more than half the length of the fleet carriers of the time and less than a third the weight. They were armed with four double 40mm and fifteen single 20mm anti-aircraft guns, as well as two four-inch anti-aircraft guns. The layout of the CVE included an "island" that was quite small and located well forward of the funnel, as opposed to that of the larger fleet carrier whose funnel was integrated into the island. The early examples of CVEs were equipped with a single aircraft elevator; later versions had an elevator fore and aft and a single aircraft catapult. They used the same system of landing aircraft with arresting cables and tailhooks as the big carriers and the same launch and recovery procedures.

Crew personnel aboard the CVE numbered about a third that of the larger fleet carrier. The CVE was furnished with a canteen or snack bar known as the "ge-dunk", after the sound made by its vending machines when operated. The gedunk was open longer hours than the ship's mess. There the sailors could buy ice cream, cigarettes and other consumable items.

At Ingalls yard in Mississippi, a CVE was being produced every month. Getting them delivered to the fleet of the Royal Navy was not quite as simple and direct, however. Delivery delays of up to six months were common in getting the CVEs from Mississippi to duty with the Royal Navy against the U-boats of Admiral Dönitz, with eight-month delays for the escort carriers then being built on the U.S. west coast. The CVEs had to undergo sea trials before being released for the long trip through the Panama Canal and up to the American east coast port of Norfolk, Virginia, where they were loaded to capacity with new fighter and other aircraft types being sent to U.S. units in Britain and North Africa. Often, they were delayed several weeks awaiting the assembly of a convoy in which to make the perilous Atlantic crossing. At times they had to stop at Casablanca to off-load aircraft before continuing on to England, which then added as much as three more weeks to the journey . . . which wasn't over yet. Once they had arrived in England, they had to spend up to eight more weeks in a dockyard there for completion of modifications to make them fully ready for combat. The British required several significant alterations which included a lengthening of the flight deck to accommodate certain of their aircraft, such as the Fairey Swordfish which could not use the American catapult launch system and needed extra take-off distance.

As additional British modifications were added to the Lend-Lease CVEs, to enhance their capabilities beyond the anti-submarine role, all the various delays were brought to the attention of U.S. Navy Chief of Staff Admiral Ernest King who was told by the Allied Anti-Submarine Survey Board that he should retain five out of the next batch of seven Lend-Lease escort carriers, for use by the U.S. Navy. He then learned from the British Admiralty that the delays were being compounded by congestion in the UK dockyards as the work on the modifications to the CVEs was backing up, and becoming more and more backed up with the continuing arrival of new CVEs from the United States. They also told him that they were having problems manning all the new escort carriers. Knowing that his own U.S. Navy was probably even less able to man the CVEs in question at that point, King urged the British to urgently look for ways to reduce the delays at their end, which they did.

The uses of the escort carriers in the service of the United States Navy evolved through the war years into a greater range of roles than had originally been intended. In the bitter reaches of the North Atlantic, for example, their value increased dramatically when they began to supplement the activity of the escorting destroyers in providing vital air support for the anti-submarine warfare. In one historic incident, the escort carrier USS *Guadalcanal* played a major part in the capture of the German submarine *U-505* off North Africa in 1944. The CVEs lacked sufficient speed to run with the fast carrier attack groups, and were frequently assigned to escort the troop carriers and landing ships in the intensive island-hopping campaign across the Pacific. In so doing they provided air cover for the troopships, flying the initial wave of beach attacks during the amphibious landing operations. At times they

above: The Royal Navy's American-built escort carrier HMS *Pursuer.*

were called on to escort the large carriers, to act as emergency landing facilities when their big sisters were tied up refueling and rearming their own aircraft. They filled another vital role too in carrying aircraft and spare parts from various ports in the United States to remote island airstrips.

But the peak of the action for the escort carriers in the Second World War may have been in the Battle off Samar in the Philippines on 25 October 1944. The action began when U.S. Navy Admiral William F. "Bull" Halsey, Jr. was lured by the Japanese Navy into chasing a decoy enemy fleet with his powerful American 3rd Fleet. His decision meant that the aircraft of his sixteen small, slow escort carriers—aircraft armed with bombs for ground support activity—were left with just a small force of destroyers and destroyer escorts to fight a huge main force of Japanese battleships, one of which was the giant *Yamato,* together with eight cruisers and eleven destroyers. Amazingly, though, thanks largely to the extraordinarily aggressive attacks of the American screening ships, the escort carriers were able to turn back the enemy attacking force. In the battle, the slow escort carriers were forced to launch their planes and then maneuver in the area for more than an hour, receiving many hits from the armour-piercing shells of the enemy cruisers. Most of those shells passed through the thin, unar-

above left: U.S. Navy Fleet Admiral Ernest J. King, Chief of Naval Operations; above right: Lt Commander Morris Montgomery, survivor of the *Gambier Bay* sinking, and his granddaughter, Naval Flight Officer Shannon Callahan.

moured hulls without exploding. One major casualty of the decisive Battle of Leyte Gulf, however, was the escort carrier USS *Gambier Bay*, the only American carrier to be lost to gunfire in the war. The battle involved 321 warships and 1,996 aircraft, more ships and planes than in any other battle in naval history, and virtually eliminated the Japanese fleet as an effective offensive force in the war.

By summer 1944, Japan had lost their offensive position in much of the Pacific. They knew that the Americans were getting ready to invade the Philippines and believed it essential that Japanese military forces keep possession and control of the island group. Without it, they would lose the oil and other supplies and raw materials coming from Sumatra, which would end their war effort and threaten their survival. They believed that the American invading force would come through the Leyte Gulf and they determined to fight what they foresaw as one of the greatest naval battles in history there.

The keel of the *Gambier Bay* had been laid at Kaiser Shipbuilding in Vancouver, Washington, on 10 July 1943. She had been named for a small bay on Admiralty Island, Alaska. Following her commissioning on 28 December at Astoria, Oregon, she was taken to San Diego on her shakedown cruise before sailing for Pearl Harbor and the Marshall Islands in February 1944, where she delivered eighty-four replacement aircraft for the fleet carrier *Enterprise*. She then returned to Pearl to pick up battle-damaged planes and bring them back to the U.S. for repairs. While in San Diego again, she was laid up in drydock to correct a major vibration problem she had developed crossing the Pacific. By March she was at sea again supporting U.S. Marine Corsair pilots in their carrier qualifications.

Gambier Bay sailed again for the Marshall Islands in early May, a part of Task Group 52.11 which was preparing for the American invasion of the Marianas Islands, where, from the U.S. B-29 bomber bases on Tinian, the Japanese home islands would receive the final bombs of the war. During the Marianas invasion, aircraft from *Gambier Bay* flew many close air support missions for the Marine landings, downing several enemy aircraft. Further such activity followed at Guam, Peleliu and Angaur, and after that the escort carrier escorted troop transports and amphibious landing craft to Leyte Gulf for the impending invasion of the Philippines. She was now part of Task Group 77, code-named Taffy 3, under the command of Admiral Thomas L. Sprague. In it she would be operating with other escort carriers including USS *Kitkun Bay*, USS *Kalinin Bay*, USS *Fanshaw Bay*, USS *St. Lo*, and the USS *White Plains*.

The American task group encountered that large Japanese warship force in the early morning of 25 October 1944. Captain Walter Vieweg, the skipper of *Gambier Bay*, was awakened at 2.30 a.m. by his communications watch officer, informing the captain that the Battle of Surigao Straits was under way, causing him to order that torpedoes be loaded on all his uncommitted Avenger aircraft. At 7 a.m. Captain Vieweg received a report from the task group anti-submarine patrol that a large force of Japanese warships—four battleships, eight cruisers and thirteen destroyers—was just twenty-five miles northwest of the American warship formation, which was then heading on a southerly course. Suddenly, several salvoes of large-calibre shells began falling into the centre of the American formation, which then quickly turned eastward into the wind in order to launch aircraft. Captain Vieweg ordered that all *Gambier Bay's* planes be launched immediately to prevent their being lost should an enemy shell cause a fire on his flight deck. All seventeen of the aircraft took off safely. With their departure, he ordered the aircraft on the hangar deck brought up to the flight deck, but the task group was now turning on a more southerly heading, out of the wind, which would deny his heavily-loaded and fully fueled torpedo planes minimal conditions to launch. As they now could not be safely launched, some of his planes had to be jettisoned overboard for the safety of the ship, and the enemy salvoes were now falling much closer to the carrier. 7.30 a.m. The American destroyers were kept busy attacking the warships of the Japanese fleet, and all the American ships in the area were making smoke for their protection. A lashing rain squall had arisen as dozens of American planes, many of them without bombs and with inappropriate ordnance for the present need, continued making attacks on the enemy ships.

By 8.30 a.m. the rain had stopped. All of the American destroyers and destroyer escorts were now fully engaged in the battle and were laying smoke screens. Out on the windward edge of the escort carrier formation, both *Gambier Bay* and *Kalinin Bay* were being subjected to the heavy gunfire of the four nearest enemy cruisers. To this point, much of the enemy heavy gunfire had been somewhat innaccurate, with salvoes widely spaced, the lag time allowing *Gambier Bay* to dodge many of them. But as the distance between the carrier and the Japanese cruisers continued to decrease, the accuracy and intensity of the enemy gunfire improved considerably. Then the shells began falling onto her flight deck and near her engine room. Her speed was reduced to eleven knots and she was no longer able to maintain her position in the formation. With the enemy cruisers less than 10,000 yards distant, they were scoring consistent hits and significant damage to the carrier. For more than an hour, at least half

Warships burning in the Battle of Leyte Gulf in October 1944.

of the many shells the Japanese warships were lobbing at the carrier were scoring hits. *Gambier Bay* was experiencing considerable flooding and was essentially dead in the water, and she had no water pressure with which to fight the many fires. Captain Vieweg knew his ship could not be saved and he ordered her abandoned just before 9 a.m. as the Japanese ships continued to send shells into her. *Gambier Bay* rolled over and sank at 9.10 a.m. In addition to the carrier, her sister ship *St. Lo*, two American destroyers and a destroyer escort were also sunk in the action that morning. The other escort carriers involved were all damaged and the light carrier USS *Princeton* was sunk after being hit by two bombs from a Japanese Judy aircraft. The massive resulting fire led to the ship having to be scuttled. The losses of the Japanese were considerably heavier: four fleet aircraft carriers, three battleships, six heavy cruisers, four light cruisers, eleven destroyers, one destroyer transport, and four submarines. American losses amounted to one light aircraft carrier, two escort carriers, and three destroyers. 150 Japanese aircraft were lost, against 100 for the Americans. Personnel losses amounted to 10,000 Japanese, and 1,500 Americans.

Lieutenant Commander Morris Montgomery, USN (Ret) had served as the leading Chief Petty Officer of Composite Squadron 10, embarked in the USS *Gambier Bay* during the battle off Samar on 25 October 1944. "On the night before the ship was lost, one of the two tractors on the flight deck somehow tumbled down the elevator opening and landed on a fighter on the hangar deck. The damage was such that the plane required an engine change and the maintenance crew worked all night changing it.

"Our chief ordnance man, Andy Andrews, who bunked near me, was awakened early in the morning and I knew something was up when I heard about loading torpedoes. Our planes had previously been loaded with general purpose bombs for a land-bombing mission the following day. To reload them with torpedoes meant bringing them below to the hangar deck and disarming and defueling them, a time-consuming operation. At about 6:30 a.m., Chief Horten, the aircraft maintenance chief, and I went to the flight deck to relieve the maintenance crew who were preparing to ground-run the new engine that had been installed in the fighter that had been damaged on the elevator. They went to breakfast, Chief Horten got into the cockpit, and I stood by with a CO2 fire bottle. The engine would not run on its engine-driven pump, which was used mainly for starting and then switched off. We decided to complete the ground-run using the booster pump and change the engine pump later during the post-engine-run inspection.

"At that moment the ship was surrounded by rain squalls, but was not actually in one. During the engine-run, I noticed one of our morning anti-submarine patrol planes approaching the ship and signalling with its wings. I then saw a big splash in the water about 100 yards to port. At first I thought that the aircraft was in trouble and had jettisoned its depth charges. Then I saw a Japanese battleship emerging from a rain squall on our port horizon and heard the roar of its guns. The sound of the enemy shells passing overhead reminded me of a train passing a crossing at great speed.

"Things began to happen. People were running around; 'General Quarters' was sounded and the ship began to make screening smoke and take evasive action. Pilots began scrambling for any available aircraft. One made for the fighter with the new engine, and we told him that the booster pump was all he would have. He acknowledged and was subsequently launched. New aircraft engines had to be operated at minimum power for at least ten hours, with no combat or military power settings. The pilot eventually experienced engine failure and had to ditch.

"I could see a formation of enemy ships to our port side, seemingly at point blank range. It was a mad scramble to get our planes launched. Some were not completely refueled after the switch of ordnance, and I know that some had no ordnance. At least one was catapulted without the crew, just to get it off the ship. Either it had been 'down' mechanically or had not been refueled. The fueling system was then secured, as was normally done at 'General Quarters'. 'Dead' planes and aviation gas in the fuel risers are definitely a disadvantage in a situation such as the one we were experiencing.

"Each time the ship received a hit, footing became difficult to maintain and the generators were knocked off line, cutting the power and lights momentarily. One hit jammed our elevator, trapping those planes that were on the hangar deck.

"Once flight operations had ceased, my job on the flight deck was finished and I had no other assignments. I went to the ready room. There were several pilots there and I asked 'What the hell was happening?' One pilot said that the fleet must have all been sunk and that we were all that was left. He thought that we had not been truthfully informed as to how the war had really been going for us.

"I grabbed a Mae West life jacket and left to help out wherever I could. Men were fighting fires everywhere. I remembered that I had not put the flame cover over my bunk that morning, I went below to the CPO berthing space. The quarters contained an emergency first aid station which also served as our writing table, and it doubled as an operating table, having special lights mounted above it. When I entered, the quarters were ankle-deep in water, possibly from a broken main. A medical crew was

left: Construction in progress on the escort carrier USS *Gambier Bay* in the Second World War; above: The TBF Avenger torpedo bomber built by Grumman.

working on an injured man, and the lights were periodically blinking off and on. They had battle lanterns in use and it was an eerie sight.

"I kept a picture of my wife in a pocket-sized copy of the New Testament under my pillow. I put the bible in my shirt pocket, spread the flame cover over my bunk and went back to the flight deck. I attempted to assist the damage control crew in 'Officer Country' below the flight deck up near the bow. They had all the help they needed, so three other men and I headed up the bow when the ship received another hit. The men ahead of me seemed to disintegrate, and I was knocked down. I got up and headed back towards the Officers' quarters, where I met Lt. Bell. He was getting ready to abandon ship, and he ducked back into his room and offered me a drink from a bottle he had. We all started towards the port railing on the bow.

"The water was filled with men. I never did hear the word to abandon ship, but I knew that the end was near because the ship was dead in the water and beginning to list. I overheard the leader of one of the damage repair parties say that the magazines were being flooded. I went to the railing and then loosened the straps of my battle helmet. Training lectures had taught me to do this to avoid being injured upon entering the water. I now had a Mae West, a life belt, and a kapok life jacket which I had found on the bow. Shells were hitting, leaving various colours from their dye markers on top of the water. I went over the side.

"I hit the water and surfaced near one of our pilots. He had a mattress so I joined him. I never saw Lt. Bell again. I was glad I had gone over the port side as the tide was pushing against the starboard side. We were being carried away from the ship, unlike those men who had gone over the starboard side and were forced to follow along the ship's hull and drift off the stern.

"As we drifted away, we were constantly splashed by water from nearby shell hits. A few yards off the stern were several men in one of the large donut-type floats which had water and rations stored in them. They were waving and yelling for people to come over to them as they had plenty of room.

We began paddling in their direction. About then there was a terrific explosion, probably on the hangar deck, because the elevator (which had been jammed) came flying out of the ship and landed near us. I am certain that some men must have been struck by it when it hit the water. The float that we were heading for must have received a direct hit, for as we neared it there was a big splash, and then it wasn't there anymore. We continued to drift away from the ship and shells continued to fall near us. We began to think that the enemy gunners were using our mattress as a marker. Of course they were not, but one's reasoning in such situations is not always the best. So we abandoned the mattress and swam away from it. We soon came upon some men who were trying to spread out one of the ship's large floating nets. Such nets are unwieldy, requiring men on all sides of it, but it makes a very effective piece of life-saving equipment. By keeping the net spread out, those in the middle of it could remain about waist deep in water and have their feet supported. We put the more seriously wounded in the net. We spotted a man floating near the net and swam over to him. He was dead. He could have been a mess cook or a striker, because he was young and was wearing whites and was non-rated. We took his I.D. tags and gave them to the senior officer in our group. The *Gambier Bay* rolled over bottoms-up revealing many holes in the bottom before it sank.

"We could see a Japanese cruiser which appeared to be dead in the water. Smoke was billowing from its after section, and a Japanese destroyer was trying to assist it. At about 1300 hours we saw many planes flying in the direction of the Japanese fleet. We identified them as ours. We all shouted and waved our arms, and several of us yelled 'they went thataway'. We were in pretty good spirits at that time. Later we thought how fortunate we were that the Japanese force had gone before our planes arrived. Otherwise, we might have been hit during the bombing attack. I remember seeing the Japanese cruiser burning just before dark. It may have sunk during the night, as there were several underwater explosions.

"It was a very cold night, especially if any part of your body became exposed to the air. The water was a bit rough and we were constantly being drenched with salt water. We tied ourselves together with the attachment strings on our life jackets. That way, if you fell asleep or dozed off, you wouldn't drift away. One of the wounded men had a large piece of metal stuck in his back, apparently wedged so tightly that he was only bleeding slightly. The doctor said not to pull it out or else he might bleed to death. We took turns holding his head up out of the water and trying to comfort him. On the second day, as I was holding him, he began to talk about things back in his childhood. As the day wore on he became incoherent. Finally, he went into a coma and died, possibly from shock and internal bleeding. We took his I.D. tags and gave him a burial prayer. We then allowed his body to drift away and sink.

"We had about ninety men in and around our net. Everyone was getting thirsty and hungry. At one point I heard two men talking. I don't know if they were joking or temporarily out of their heads. One of them said that his father owned the bar around the corner and if the other one would go with him, he would set up the drinks. They both paddled around to the other side of the net and began to drink salt water. The men near them promptly stopped them from doing so. Those of us who were not severely wounded and had control of themselves would watch for men attempting to drink salt water and kept others from swimming away. During that time, one's mind would play tricks and you would see objects like mirages, or imagine things. I saw a fleet of rescue ships, or so I thought, until someone shook me. In the night, as I was dozing, one of the men near me began pounding me on the head and screaming that I was trying to get ahead of him in the chow line. We prayed frequently for rescue, food, and water.

"Later, a few of us spotted something bobbing on the horizon. It turned out to be Chief McArdle towing two wounded men. One of them was Forest Khort and the other was Denard, both from our squadron. They had a small water breaker and part of a can of emergency rations. Malt tablets. We helped them to our net and rigged a drinking hose from one of our Mae West inflation hoses to a spigot on the water breaker. We all received a small sip of water and one malt tablet. A 2nd Class Storekeeper from our group took charge of the water and rations and did the rationing. We saw to the wounded men in the middle of the net first. I don't claim to be any more religious than the next man, but it was at this point that my faith in God was most profound, and I then had faith that we would be rescued.

"We lost several men, mostly from just drifting away or taking off on their own. At first we would swim out and bring them back, but near the end of our time in the water, we didn't have the strength to do this any more. We learned later that some of the men who had left our group had eventually floated into another group.

"Most of us were badly sunburned from the glare off the water. On the second day we found a floating drum of oil and we smeared some of the oil on all of us, but it was a little too late. My lips were raw and bleeding and felt like they stood out a foot in front of me. At that point my Mae West had lost most of its air and the inflation hose had clogged with congealed fuel oil. My kapok life jacket was partially water-logged. On the first day in the water I had given my life belt to someone who needed one. One of the ship's warrant officers had found a wooden gangway post and, realizing the condition of my life-saving equipment, I joined him, each of us clinging to an end of the post. We had good manoeuvrability and were supported somewhat. To be able to support one's dangling weight just a little bit was a tremendous relief. Our life jackets were becoming water-logged, causing us to sink further into the water. As the seas got heavier, the float net kept trying to roll up, and it was a real chore keeping it straightened and spread out. The sea state was becoming worse and ominous clouds were forming. It began to worry us. We stayed near the net, our legs quite numb from dangling in the water.

"On our second night in the water we spotted what we thought was Samar Island in the distance and had to decide whether to risk the possibility of drifting ashore there. We reasoned that it was enemy-held, but we decided that it was our best chance for survival and we thought that some of the wounded men would not survive another day in the water, so we began to try to control our drift towards the island.

"Just before daybreak we saw some short sweeps of searchlights, on and off. Someone thought that they might be Japanese torpedo boats. We finally agreed to try to indicate our position. We yelled and blew the whistles attached to our life jackets and we were suddenly engulfed in the beam of a search-light and I could see an American sailor near the light source. It was the most welcome sight of my life. The men on board the craft began tossing out heaving lines and putting out litter-type stretchers wrapped with life jacktes for bouyancy for the wounded. I was hauled up on deck and my oil-soaked clothes were cut away. I said: 'I'm OK. I can make it', and when they released me my legs just folded up and down I went. They carried me below. Naked, oily men were stacked up like a fresh-caught load of fish. Apparently they had picked up other groups of survivors before us. Someone gave me a small sip of water and, a minute or so later, another one, and so on. My lips were so swollen and painful, and my tongue so raw and ulcerated from constantly spitting out the salt water, that I actually cried when the cup came close, but my desire for water was stronger than the ensuing pain. Other than a little soup, the first food we were given was pancakes, they looked and smelled delicious and I very much wanted to eat them. I became quite frustrated, but the pain was just too great and I had to forego the meal.

"Eventually we made it to Leyte Harbor, which was filled with troop transport and utility ships. I was transferred to an LST (Landing Ship Tank) that had been converted to an emergency hospital ship, and was examined, treated and released as an ambulatory patient. I was suffering from severe shortness of breath, diagnosed as resulting from concussion. I had various cuts and bruises, severe sunburn and other effects from exposure. I was one of the lucky ones."

above: American Naval Flight Officers in training at NAS Pensacola, Florida, in a dunking device designed to replicate the experience of having to escape from a submerged aircraft

Midway

U.S. Navy carrier-based pilots are briefed aboard the USS *Enterprise* for a mission.

The excellent military historian Sir John Keegan referred to the Battle of Midway as "the most stunning and decisive blow in the history of naval warfare." After it, the balance of sea power and sea-borne air power in the Pacific theater of the war shifted dramatically from the Japanese to the Americans. It was unquestionably the most important naval battle of the campaign. Occurring between 4 and 7 June 1942, just six months after the Japanese attack on American ships and facilities at Pearl Harbor, Hawaii, American forces wrought irreparable damage on the Japanese fleet in the worst naval defeat that nation had experienced in 350 years.

In their planning and preparation for the battle, the Japanese were seeking to destroy the American fleet as a strategic power in the Pacific and in so doing, achieve a free hand for themselves in furthering their stated determination to develop their Greater East Asia Co-Prosperity Sphere, the means to their own total domination of the Pacific region. Their Midway plan called for luring the fleet aircraft carriers of the U.S. Navy into a trap and occupying Midway Island as a prime factor in extending a Japanese defensive perimeter, following the American attack led by Lt Col. Jimmy Doolittle on Tokyo in April 1942. In that raid sixteen B-25 Mitchell bombers took off from the U.S. aircraft carrier *Hornet* to bomb targets in the Japanese capitol and other cities. While doing little meaningful damage, the raid dealt an extreme psychological blow to the Japanese people and military leadership, underscoring the significant gap in the defences of their home islands.

American codebreakers, however, were able to intercept vital aspects of the Midway plan, the date and location of the intended attack, enabling the U.S. Navy to establish an ambush of its own.

In the battle, four of the six Japanese fleet aircraft carriers that had participated in the raid on Pearl Harbor, the *Akagi, Kaga, Hiryu,* and *Soryu,* were sunk, as was a heavy cruiser. American losses included one carrier, the USS *Yorktown,* and one destroyer.

The Battle of Midway not only turned the tide of the Pacific war; but with the attrition in manpower and equipment suffered by the Japanese in their Solomon Islands campaign, and their inability to maintain the necessary pace in replacing their warship and pilot losses after Midway, these key factors and America's ability to keep increasing her wartime industrial output and pilot training sealed Japan's fate in the remainder of the conflict.

"There set out, slowly, for a Different World. At four, on winter mornings, different legs . . . You can't break eggs without making an omelette—that's what they tell the eggs."
—from *A War* by Randall Jarrell

In the evening of 3 June 1942, the U.S. Navy aircraft carrier *Hornet* (CV-8) was steaming towards a large force of Japanese warships near the Pacific island of Midway. Earlier that day, a small force of U.S. Army Air Corps B-17 Flying Fortress bombers based on Midway had attacked some of these warships of the Japanese task force, setting fire to two of them. Now the pilots of Torpedo Squadron Eight were gathering in their ready room aboard the *Hornet* to learn about the plan of attack they would take part in when the two opposing forces met. As the briefing began, their Lt Commander John Waldron handed out mimeographed copies of his final message to them ahead of what would become known as the Battle of Midway: "Just a word to let you know that I feel we are all ready. We have had a very short time to train and we have worked under the most severe difficulties. But we have truly done the best humanly possible. I actually believe that under these conditions we are the best in the

far left: Final assembly of Douglas SBD Dauntless dive-bombers at El Segundo, California plant; centre left: U.S. Navy Fleet Admiral Chester W. Nimitz, Commander-in-Chief U.S. Pacific Fleet; left: A poster recognizing the contribution of 'Rosie the Riveter', the women war workers of America in WW2; below: A Grumman F4F Wildcat fighter ready for take-off from a U.S. Navy carrier in WW2.

world. My greatest hope is that we encounter a favorable tactical situation, but if we don't, and the worst comes to the worst, I want each of us to do his utmost to destroy our enemies. If there is only one plane left to make a final run-in, I want that man to go in and get a hit. May God be with us all. Good luck, happy landings, and give 'em hell."

A letter to his wife from Commander Waldron: "Dear Adelaide, There is not a bit of news that I can tell you now except that I am well. I have yours and the children's pictures here with me all the time and I think of you most of the time.

"I believe that we will be in battle very soon. I wish we were there today. But, as we are up to the very eve of serious business, I wish to record to you that I am feeling fine. My own morale is excellent, and from my continued observation of the squadron, their morale is excellent also. You may rest assured that I will go in with the expectation of coming back in good shape. If I do not come back, you and the little girls can know that this squadron struck for the highest objective in Naval warfare— to sink the enemy. "I hope this letter will not scare you, and, of course, if I have a chance to write another to be mailed at the same time as this, then of course I shall do so.

"I love you and the children very dearly and I long to be with you. But, I could not be happy ashore at this time. My place is here with the fight. I could not be happy otherwise. I know you wish me luck and I believe I will have it.

"You know, Adelaide, in this business of the torpedo attack, I acknowledge we must have a break. I believe that I have the experience, and enough Sioux in me, to profit by and recognize the break when it comes, and it will come.

"God bless you, dear. You are a wonderful wife and mother. Kiss and love the little girls for me and be of good cheer.
"Love to all from Daddy and Johnny."

And from pilot Pete Creasy, Jr: "Honey, if anything happens to me, I wish you would keep on visiting the folks, for they love you just as much as they would if you were one of their own kids. And by all means, don't become an old maid. Find someone else and make a happy home. Don't be worrying about me and I will be trying to write more often."

A signal was flashed to *Hornet* early in the morning of 4 June 1942 about an attack by four U.S. Navy PBY Catalina flying boat patrol bombers. The Catalinas had struck at enemy warships southwest of Midway. In the next two hours 'General Quarters' was sounded in *Hornet* and the pilots of Torpedo Eight again filed into their ready room. There they waited, some dozing off in the big leather chairs, while the men in charge, Admiral Marc Mitscher and the ship's captain Charles Mason, awaited confirmation of the enemy fleet's exact position. They had to be certain the distance between the U.S. carriers and the enemy fleet would be short enough to give the American pilots a safe fuel margin in the operation.

At 6 a.m. the pilots were released to the wardroom for breakfast and shortly after their meal General Quarters was sounded again and on arriving back in the ready room they learned that Midway was under attack by Japanese aircraft. One of the TBD Devastator pilots of Torpedo Eight, Ensign George Gay, recalled: "There was a real commotion as we hauled out our plotting boards, helmets, goggles, gloves, pistols, hunting knives and all our other gear. We took down the flight information.

"We had only six of our planes on the flight deck as there was no more room. And since we were to be alone anyhow, we were the last to be launched. The skipper had tried in vain to get us fighter

Manpower moving a Douglas dive-bomber on the flight deck of a U.S. Navy fleet aircraft carrier in WW2.

protection. He even tried to get one fighter to go with us, or even to get one fighter plane and one of us would fly it even though we had never been up in one, but he could not swing it. The Group Commander and the Captain felt that the SBDs needed more assitance than we did. They had caught hell in the Coral Sea [battle] and the torpedo planes had been lucky. However, the torpedo planes had made the hits in the Coral Sea, so the Japs were going to be looking for us.

"The TBD could not climb anywhere near as high as the dive-bombers needed to go, and the Group Commander and the fighter boys did not want us at two levels up there. "Under these conditions, Commander Waldron reasoned, our best bet was to be right on the water so the Zeros could not get under us. Since it was obvious that we would be late getting away, with nine of our planes still to be brought up from the hangar deck for launching, the problem would be overtaking to form a coordinated attack.

"As I went up to the flight deck, I ducked into a first aid station, got a tourniquet and put it in my pocket. As I got to the edge of the island I met the skipper coming down from the bridge. 'I'm glad I caught you', he said. 'I've been trying to convince them the Japs will not be going towards Midway—especially if they find out we are here. The Group Commander is going to take the whole bunch down there. I'm going more to the north and maybe by the time they come north and find them, we can catch up and all go in together. Don't think I'm lost. Just track me, so if anything happens to me, the boys can count on you to bring them back.'

"Each of us would be tracking, and the others all knew how to do it, but it would be my job since I was Navigation Officer. That is also the reason why I was the last man in the formation. It gave me more room to navigate instead of flying formation so closely.

"At a little before 0900 the planes started taking off, and it was 0915 when the signal man motioned me forward to the take-off position. He only had me move forward enough so that I could unfold my wings, and so I began my take-off with the tail of my plane still sitting on the number three elevator. I had more than enough room on deck in front of me to take off, and I noticed as I came back by the ship that the planes that were to follow me were being moved further up the deck with the hope of being able to bring the rest of the torpedo planes of Squadron Eight up the elevator from the hangar deck so they could get in take-off position.

"The rest of Torpedo Eight got off after what seemed to be an eternity; then we all joined up and headed away from our fleet.

"After an uneasy and uneventful hour, the skipper's voice broke radio silence" 'There's a fighter on our tail.' What he saw proved to be a Jap scout plane flying at about 1,000 feet. It flew on past us, but I knew, and I'm sure the others did, that he had seen us and reported to the Jap Navy that there were carrier planes approaching.

"We had been flying long enough now to find something, and I could almost see the wheels going around in Waldron's head. He did exactly what I had expected. He put the first section into a scouting line. Each of the eight planes was to move out into a line even with the skipper's wing tips. We had never done this before, only talked about it, and in spite of the warnings and dire threats, the fellows got too much distance between the planes. I knew immediately that this was wrong, as the planes on each end were nearly out of sight. The basic idea is OK, so that you can scan more ocean, but this was ridiculous. I thought to myself, 'Oh, no! Those guys will catch hell when we get back.'

"The skipper was upset, and he gave the join-up signal forcefully. We had just gotten together when smoke columns appeared on the horizon. In less time than it takes to tell, it became obvious that the

left: An DBD dive-bomber passing the battleship USS *Washington*. The carrier USS *Lexington* is in the background; below: A spectacular accident in which a TBM-3E Avenger torpedo bomber splinters the flight deck of the USS *Philippine Sea* in an attempted landing; centre: building Douglas SBD dive-bombers at El Segundo in southern California.

below: A Kingfisher is catapulted off on an observation flight from the battleship USS *Texas*; right: Young naval trainees at the Bainbridge, Maryland training school in the Second World War.

old Indian had taken us straight to the Japs as we could fly.

"The first capital ship I recognized as a carrier—the *Soryu*. Then I made out the *Kaga* and the *Akagi*. There was another carrier further on, and screening ships all over the damned ocean. The smoke was from what looked like a battleship, and the carriers were landing planes. The small carrier off on the horizon had smoke coming out of her also. My first thought was, 'Oh, Christ! We're late!' The skipper gave the signal for us to spread out to bracket the biggest carrier for an attack, and that was when the Zeros swarmed all over us.

"Since we had flown straight to the enemy fleet, while everyone else was looking for them, there was no one else for their air cover to worry about.

"Seeing immediately that the Zeros had us cold, the skipper signalled for us to join back together for mutual protection. We had not moved far apart, so we were back together almost immediately. The skipper broke radio silence again: 'We will go in. We won't turn back. Former strategy cannot be used. We will attack. Good luck.'

"I have never questioned the skipper's judgement or decisions. As it turned out, it didn't make any difference anyhow. We had run into a virtual trap, but we still had to do something to disrupt their

landing planes, so he took us right in. We had calculated our fuel to be very short, even insufficient to get us back to the *Hornet,* but this was not considered suicidal by any of us. We thought we had a fighting chance, and maybe after we dropped our fish we could make it to Midway. Things then started happening really fast.

"I cannot tell you the sequence in which the planes went down. Everything was happening at once, but I was consciously seeing it all. At least one plane blew up, and each would hit the water and seem to disappear. Zeros were coming in from all angles and from both sides at once. They would come in from abeam, pass each other just over our heads, and turn around to make another attack. It was evident that they were trying to get our lead planes first. The planes of Torpedo Eight were falling at irregular intervals. Some were on fire and some did a half-roll and crashed on their backs, completely out of control. Machine-gun bullets ripped my armour plate a number of times. As they rose above it, the bullets would go over my shoulder into the instrument panel and the windshield.

"Waldron was shot down very early. His plane burst into flames, and I saw him stand up to get out of the fire. He put his right leg outside the cockpit, and then hit the water and disappeared. His radioman, Dobbs, didn't have a chance. When we had been leaving Pearl Harbor, Dobbs had orders back

55

to the States to teach radio. But he had chosen to delay that assignment and stay with us.

"Much too early, it seemed, Bob Huntington [George Gay's radioman/gunner] said, 'They got me!' 'Are you hurt bad?' I asked. I looked back and Bob was slumped down almost out of sight. 'Can you move?' I asked. He said no more.

"It was while I was looking back at Bob that the plane to my left must have been shot down, because when I looked forward again it was not there. I think that was the only plane I did not actually see get hit.

"We were right on the water at full throttle and wide open, which was about 180 knots. Anyone slamming into the sea had no chance of survival—at that speed the water is just like cement. That is why I was so sure that they were all dead.

"It's hard to explain, but I think Bob being put out of action so soon was one of the things that saved me. I no longer had to fly straight and level for him to shoot, so I started dodging. I even pulled up a few times, and took some shots at Zeros as they would go by. I am positive I hit one, knocking plexiglas out of his canopy. I may have scared him, but I certainly did not hurt him personally, or even damage his plane much.

"The armour-plate bucket seat was another thing that worked well for me. I could feel, as well as hear and sometimes see, those tracer bullets. They would clunk into the airplane or clank against that armoured seat, and I had to exercise considerable control over when to kick the rudder.

"About this time I felt something hit my arm and felt it to see what it was. There was a hole in my sleeve and I got blood on my hand. I felt closer, and there was a lump under the skin of my arm. I squeezed the lump, just as you would pop a pimple, and a bullet popped out. I remember thinking, 'Well, what do you know—a souvenir.' I was too busy to put it into my pocket. So I put the bullet in my mouth, blood and all, thinking, 'What the hell—it's my blood.'

"We were now in a position, those of us still left, to turn west again to intercept the ship we had chosen to attack, but the Zeros were still intent on not letting us through, and our planes kept falling all around me. We were on the ship's starboard side, or to the right and ahead of our target, and as we closed range the big carrier began to turn towards us. I knew immediately from what the skipper had said so often in his lectures, that if she got into a good turn she could not straighten out right away, and I was glad that she had committed herself. At that moment there were only two planes left of our squadron besides my own. One was almost directly ahead of me, but off a bit to my left. I skidded to the left and avoided more 20mm slugs just in time to pull my nose up and fire at another Zero as he got in front of me. I only had one .30 caliber gun, and although I knew I hit this Zero also, it did little damage. When I turned back to the right, the plane that had been directly ahead of me was gone, and the other one was out of control.

"My target, which I think was the *Kaga*, was now in a hard turn to starboard and I was going towards her forward port quarter. I figured that by the time a torpedo could travel the distance it should be in the water, the ship should be broadside. I aimed about one-quarter of the ship's length ahead of her bow, and reached out with my left hand to pull back the throttle. It had been calculated that we should be at about eighty knots when we dropped these things, so I had to slow down.

"I had just got hold of the throttle when something hit the back of my hand and it hurt like hell. My hand didn't seem to be working right, so I had to pull the throttle back mostly with my thumb. You can well imagine that I was not being exactly neat about all this; I was simply trying to do what I had come out to do. When I figured that I had things about as good as I was going to get them, I

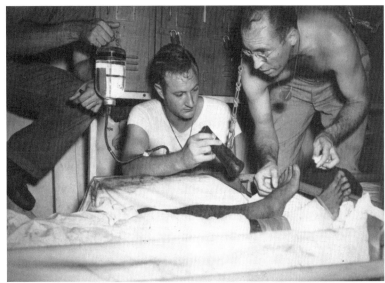

above: Ensign George Gay, a TBD Devastator pilot of Torpedo Squadron Eight; right: Treating a wounded airman at sea.

punched the torpedo release button. Nothing happened.

"'Damn those tracers' I thought.'They've goofed up my electrical release and I'm getting inside my range.' I had been told that the ideal drop was 1,000 yards range, eighty knots speed and eighty feet or so of altitude. But by the time I got the control stick between my knees and put my left hand on top of it to fly the plane, and reached across to pull the cable release with my good right hand, I was in to about 850 yards. The cable, or mechanical release, came out of the instrument panel on the left side, designed to be pulled with the left hand, but those damned Zeros had messed up my program. My left hand did not work. It was awkward and I almost lost control of the plane trying to pull out that cable by the roots. I can't honestly say I got rid of that torpedo. It felt like it. I had never done it before so I couldn't be sure, and with the plane pitching like a bronco, I had to be content with trying my best.

"God, but that ship looked big! I remember thinking.'Why in the hell doesn't the *Hornet* look that big when I'm trying to land on her?'

"I remember that I did not want to fly out over the starboard side and let all those gunners have a chance at me, so I headed out over the stern.

"I thought,'I could crash into all this and make one great big mess, maybe even get myself a whole carrier, but I'm feeling passably good, and my plane is still flying, so the hell with that—I'll keep going. Maybe I'll get another crack at them and do more damage in the long run.'

"Flying as low as I could, I went between a couple of cruisers and out past the destroyers. If you have ever seen movies of this sort of thing, you may wonder how anything could get through all that gunfire. I am alive to tell you that it can be done. I think my plane was hit a few times . . .

"The Zeros had broken off me when I got into ack-ack, but they had no trouble going around to meet me on the other side. A 20mm cannon slug hit my left rudder pedal just outside my little toe, blew the pedal apart and knocked a hole in the firewall. This set the engine on fire, and it was burning my left leg through that hole.

"When the rudder pedal went, the control wire to the ailerons and the rudder went with it. I [still] had the elevators, so I could pull the nose up. Reaching over with my right hand, I cut the switch. That was also on the left side. I was able to hold the nose up and slow down to almost a decent ditching speed.

"Most airplanes will level out if you turn them loose, especially if they are properly trimmed. Mine was almost making it, but I was crosswind, so the right wing hit first. This slammed me into the water in a cartwheel fashion and banged the hood shut over me before it twisted the frame and jammed the hood tight.

"As I unbuckled, water was rising to my waist. The nose of the plane was down, so I turned around and sat on the instrument panel while trying to get that hood open. It wouldn't budge. When that water got up to my armpits and started lapping at my chin, I got scared—and I mean really scared. I knew the plane would dive as soon as it lost buoyancy and I didn't want to drown in there. I panicked, stood up and busted my way out.

"The Zeros were diving and shooting at me but my first thought now was of Bob Huntington, I was almost positive he was dead. I think he took at least one of those cannon slugs right in the chest, but I thought that the water might revive him and I had to try and help him. I got back to him just as the plane took that dive, and I went down with it trying to unbuckle his straps and get him out.

"The beautiful water exploded into a deep red, and I lost sight of everything. What I had seen confirmed my opinion of his condition and I had to let Bob go. The tail took a gentle swipe at me as if to say goodbye and I came up choking. I lost the bullet from my mouth and as I watched it sink in that blue, clear water, I grabbed for it but missed. Zeros were still strafing me and I ducked under a couple of times as those thwacking slugs came close. As I came up for air once, I bumped my head on my life raft out of the plane."

George Gay was the only member of Torpedo Eight to survive their attack that day. With his wits and luck, he evaded capture by the ships of the enemy fleet that drove past him as he floated near them, his head covered by a thin black seat cushion that had emerged from his sinking plane, along with a four-man life raft. That entire afternoon, in the presence of the Japanese warships, he "rode" that uninflated raft like a horse, concealing it and himself from his foes, having to wait until nightfall to inflate it.

From his vantage point, he watched the destruction of three great carriers of the enemy fleet, by the dive-bombers of *Hornet* and the other U.S. flattops. After about thirty hours in the water, Gay was saved when he was sighted by a PBY crew who landed nearby to pick him up.

He was flown to Midway and later to Pearl Harbor where a doctor examined him and noted that the ensign had lost roughly a pound an hour in body weight during his time in the sea.

While recovering, George Gay was visited in his hospital room by Admiral Chester W. Nimitz, Commander-in-Chief of the U.S. Pacific Fleet. The admiral had a more than casual interest in the ensign's account of what he had observed in the course of his amazing adventure. Gay later received the Navy Cross and the Purple Heart.

Paddles

A World War Two landing signal officer brings a naval aviator aboard the carrier.

right: A Douglas AD Skyraider in a landing accident aboard a U.S. Navy carrier in the Korean War; right: A Vought Corsair fighter arrives aboard the American aircraft carrier USS *Tarawa*, an *Essex* class carrier, in the western Pacific.

In the British Royal Navy he was known as the batsman; in the U.S. Navy he was referred to as the landing signal officer. For a large part of the existence of aircraft carriers he has had responsibility for guiding aviators onto the flight deck to a safe landing or "trap." Over the years the job and the technology have evolved and in the American navy each squadron in the air wing of each carrier had its own landing signal officer—a fellow pilot—to help his colleagues down the landing approach. When a landing pilot is doing everything correctly, the LSO will keep his communication to a minimum. If corrections are needed he will signal the pilot or talk him down with what the pilots refer to as "candy calls" as the pilot makes the appropriate adjustments to the approach. When a pilot over-corrects, under-corrects, or fails to make the required adjustments in his approach to the deck, he receives a wave-off from the LSO. The wave-off sends the pilot around to rejoin the landing pattern for another try. The wave-off is non-negotiable and must be obeyed.

The aircraft recovery system used on the carriers of the U.S. Navy involves a carrier air traffic control center (CATCC) which guides returning aircraft to the carrier control area around the ship. It clears each aircraft for an approach to a landing at one-minute intervals in various weather conditions. In normal visual landing conditions the skill and experience of the landing signal officer enters the frame. The LSO is a highly experienced naval aviator of exceptional skill as a carrier pilot. He has a proven record, evaluated and well-trained at Landing Signal Officer school and on the carrier. To qualify for the job, he or she has demonstrated sensitivity, the wisdom of experience, and good judgement. The office is a small platform near the landing area, on the aft port side of the carrier flight deck. Using state-of-the-art equipment, with assistants and LSOs in training, he continuously monitored the

weather conditions, wind, the motion of the deck, and the characteristics of operating aircraft, in addition to thoughtfully considering the experience level of each approaching pilot.

Under normal visual flying conditions, the carrier-based aircraft return from missions and are sometimes placed in a marshal stack in which flight leaders take their interval on flights at lower altitude levels in the stack. As the mission aircraft approach astern of the carrier, either two- or four-plane formations enter the break for landing, on the same heading and to the starboard side at an altitude of 800 feet. When the flight leader reaches a projected point ahead of the carrier, he breaks left and aligns his airplane on a downwind leg, while descending to 600 feet and completing his landing checklist. On final approach the pilot will rely on the ship's automatic, gyrostabilized Fresnel lens optical landing system, which is an arrangement of lenses and lights positioned off the port edge of the angled flight deck. Should the carrier be rolling and/or pitching beyond the limitations of the gyrostabilization capability—or if the Fresnel system should fail—a manual optical visual landing system (MOVLAS) can be quickly set up for use. In reasonably good weather conditions, the LSO operates zip-lip, without radio communication.

Typically, the pilot of an F/A-18 Hornet multi-role fighter turns onto his or her final approach to the carrier deck at about 135 knots airspeed. To employ the Fresnel optical landing system, the pilot must locate the array of lights and focus on the amber light or 'meatball' in the centre of the mirrored lenses. When he has properly aligned on the glide slope he will see the ball aligned with a horizontal line of green reference lights on either side of the centre lens. If his aircraft is above the glide slope, or too high, the ball will appear to him in one of the lenses above the centre lens. If his aircraft is too low, the ball will show in one of the lower lenses. To achieve an optimal carrier landing, the pilot must

Interrogating a U.S. Navy aviator after flying a mission from the carrier USS *Enterprise* in WW2.

visually keep the ball centred all the way down the glide slope to touchdown on the flight deck and then engage the three wire, the third of four heavy cables stretched across the aft area of the flight deck from just ahead of the ramp or rounded aft end of the deck. The pilot must learn to fly the ball. The LSO will help with light signals and/or voice instruction.

In the landing approach to the deck, the pilot flies his aircraft to a point about three-quarters of a mile from the ship. At that point the ship's air traffic control centre delegates control of the aircraft to the LSO. It is then that the LSO and his or her half dozen assistants, some of whom are training their binoculars on the incoming jet, checking that the landing gear and flaps are in the proper down position, the airplane is aligned on the centreline of the flight deck, the wings are level, and the plane appears to be descending at a correct rate to catch one of the arresting wires when it slams onto the deck in a few seconds.

To bring a hot, heavy beast like an F/A-18 aboard a carrier is a highly precise, demanding task and there is little room for error. The pilot has to establish the airplane's position and attitude on the glide slope and then fly it down the slope at an exact three-and-a-half degree angle. When the airplane arrives over the ramp, if the pilot has flown the glide slope perfectly, the tailhook will cross the ramp fourteen feet above it. If the plane is more than a few feet too high, the tailhook will miss the arresting wires, or bounce over them, for what is called a 'bolter'. Navy procedure requires the pilot to shove the throttle (throttles in the case of a multi-engine aircraft) to full power the instant the airplane contacts the flight deck. When the plane's tailhook catches an arresting wire, bringing it to an abrupt halt, the pilot immediately retards the throttle and the plane is allowed to roll back a few feet to disengage the tailhook from the wire. The aircraft is then quickly guided away from the active landing area and the arresting gear is reset for the next approaching airplane. If a pilot experiences a bolter and the tailhook fails to catch an arresting wire, the plane's engine is set at full power and the plane can then get airborne again and go around for another landing attempt.

On every carrier landing approach, the LSO and the deputy LSO each hold an up-raised pickle switch and either of them can use it to activate flashing red lights on the Fresnel array, signalling a wave-off. Every landing approach to the carrier is graded by the LSO, who uses a Trend Analysis form to keep a record of every pilot's carrier landing performance. After all landings in a flight operation have been completed, members of the LSO team visit the pilots who have just landed, to discuss their grades for the task. Understandably, there are few things more important in the life of a carrier-based naval aviator than these grades. If the pilot cannot consistently and safely bring the airplane aboard the carrier, he or she is virtually worthless to the Navy and will be sent to the beach.

When an LSO gives a landing approach grade, that grade is almost always final and not subject to appeal. The grade range from: OK (a good approach with no problems), to FAIR (a performance with slight deviation from the correct approach, to NO GRADE (an unacceptable deviation from the correct approach, to WAVE-OFF (the approach was too far from correct, was unsafe and had to be aborted), to BOLTER (try again). Among U.S. Navy aviators, competition for good grades is high.

A good approach, when the pilot has done everything well, should result in the tailhook catching either the number two or number three wire; if a bit low or slow it may catch the number one wire. Both numbers one and four are less safe than two and three, three being the most desirable.

Landing on a carrier at night, a night trap, is one of the most dangerous things a human being can do. Nothing that a pilot must do requires greater skill, is more demanding or genuinely frightening. Poor performance in night carrier landings is the biggest cause of naval aviators losing their wings. Some naval aviators say that, even after hundreds of night traps, they never get easier, and some feel that the more night landings they do, the more nervous and uneasy they are about them. One F/A-18 pilot commented: "Doing a night trap concentrates the mind wonderfully." The problem for pilots doing night traps is the lack of visual cues. When landing on a conventional airfield at night, the pilot usually has a whole range of them with which to judge the quality of his or her approach, but nighttime at sea is black on black. Frequently, there is no horizon, making the experience even more disorienting. And just setting up a proper approach can be a waking nightmare. Even so, other pilot believe that a little fear, in combination with intelligence and a high degree of capability in such a demanding situation, can actually be a good thing, one that keeps the pilot sharp and focused.

The problem of bringing an airplane to the carrier in foul weather is dealt with in various ways aboard the big *Nimitz* class carriers of the U.S. Navy. Aids availible to pilots in such conditions include the instruement landing system (ILS), the tactical air navigation system (TACAN), the carrier-controlled approach (CCA), and the automatic carrier landing system (ACLS) which is capable of bringing the plane to touchdown on the flight deck when the pilot has no visual contact with the ship much less the flight deck. A precise guidance radar in the ship locks on to the automatic pilot in the plane when it is eight miles out from the carrier. Computers in the carrier and in the plane then feed position updates to each other and the system sends signals to the plane's autopilot which establishes

below: Helicopter air-sea rescue operations from the Royal Navy carrier HMS *Illustrious*; right: A Sea Harrier landing aboard the *Illustrious*.

the approach. Using ACLS the autopilot flies the plane to a safe landing on the ship without the pilot having to touch the stick.

One of the better books to come out of the Second World War was *Daybreak for our Carrier*, by Max Miller. In it he effectively described the role of the landing signal officer on one of the fast carriers in that war: "The job aboard a carrier which appears to be the most fun (from a distance and in photographs) is that of the landing signal officer. He is the one so often pictured standing aft by the fantail, colored paddles in each hand, and waving them as if the air were rent with hornets.

"His base of operations is a small grilled platform which swings off the flight deck, and his backdrop is a screen of canvas. He doesn't stand in front of this backdrop when he is signalling, nor for that matter does he stand on the grilled platform. But they are his base of operations nevertheless, and the screen of canvas also serves as a windbreak.

"There is a slight trace of the bullfighter in a landing signal officer. He not only has to know how to lure 'em on with his colors, but he also has to know how to jump should things get too hot.

"He himself is a carrier-trained pilot. Why he was selected from regular daily flying duty to be a landing signal officer is something he most likely will avoid answering outright. It may be that he really doesn't know. Or it may be that the powers that be told him they saw in him exactly all the stuff that

U.S. Navy F/A-18 Hornet mult-
role fighters aboard the carrier
USS *John C. Stennis*.

a landing signal officer should have. And other than that, he had no say in the matter. This is the most likely.

"Planes cannot simply race in and land aboard a carrier without guiding help. They could try it, of course, and supposedly there would be some which would succeed. But on approaching the flight deck for a landing, the pilot encounters a most definite blind spot. He cannot see his own wheels at any time, of course, nor can he see the immediate spot directly beneath him and directly in front of him where his wheels should first touch. The landing signal officer has to be the other pair of eyes.

"That is one reason.

"Another reason is that, with the planes of three squadrons circling the carrier ever lower and lower for their landings, somebody has to be at a conspicuous spot to direct the timing between planes, and to see to it that the flight deck doesn't become one beautiful mess of tangled-up propellers.

"It must be remembered that a flight deck, though massive both in appearance and in actuality, is nevertheless limited in space where the planes must make their landings. This space aft with its arresting gear and barriers is less than half the deck's length. To overshoot this space, and to try to make a landing anyway, would mean to crash into the planes already aboard and which have been brought forward beyond the barriers as fast as they can be brought.

"The planes, on their approach 'in the groove,' come in at a speed of about seventy or eighty knots. At least this is the speed which is figured on if all is going well. Coupled with this, the ideal head-on wind for landing or launching planes is between thirty and forty knots. This does not mean that the wind itself has to be that strong literally. But the head-on speed of the carrier into the wind is making up for some of it.

"So, when a landing signal officer is standing out there with his colored paddles, and a plane is approaching him for a landing, he has to keep a lot of things in mind, as mentioned, and he also has to keep in mind the condition of the flight deck on his side of the barriers.

"But with his eyes concentrated on the incoming plane, and with the pilot of the plane concentrating in turn on the signal flags, it could all become quite a jumbled-up affair if the signal officer took time off to gaze at the condition of the deck behind him. He does, then, have his assistants, and one of them, an enlisted man, is the 'talker.'

"The 'talker', with earphones and a mouthpiece, squats just over the edge of the flight deck so that his eyes are level with it, and he keeps watching what is occurring to the plane which has just landed a few seconds previously.

"If there is difficultey in getting the plane released from the landing-gear, or if there is difficulty in getting the plane taxied up forward beyond the barriers, the talker's conversation to the signal officer is all one-sided. It consists of the repetition: Foul—foul—foul—foul—foul—' and then possibly a 'clear.'

"Yet it is at such point as this that a signal officer has to make one of his many split-second decisions. He is as anxious as anybody in the ship to get all the planes aboard as soon as possible. He doesn't want to give the next incoming pilot the good old 'wave-off' anymore than the incoming pilot wants to receive it.

"But if, at that critical moment of timing between speed and distance, the talker is still saying 'foul', then aloft go the signal officer's flags in criss-cross waving fashion. The pilot, in that same split second too, must push on more power to bank-turn over the deck and zoom away.

"Though pilots are obliged to take a 'wave-off' whether they like it or not, unless something devilish is the matter with their plane, they are not obliged to land even after the signal officer signals the 'cut' to do so. The signal 'cut' means, of course, to cut the motor and let the wheels touch. The signal is indicated by a quick cross whip of the flags down low. It's then up to the pilot to do the rest. The signal officer is through with him, and now looks for the next incoming plane. The 'cut' is the gesture finale with each plane, and with it the plane whirs on past the signal officer onto the deck for better or worse.

"There's a phrase which is used at times when a pilot, after getting the signal 'cut', makes a bad landing through what appears to be his own fault. So dependent has he been on the flags of the signal officer during the past few seconds that now, when suddenly on his own, the phrase is: 'He stopped flying.'

"Another job of the signal officer, as if his hands weren't filled enough, is to grade each landing much as a schoolteacher would do. This goes for the approaches as well. The moment the plane is aboard, and before the signal officer has time to forget the mental picture of the approach and of the landing, he quickly rattles off an abbreviated code of his own describing his opinion. An assistant scribbles the letters into a notebook after the pilot's name or after the number of the pilot's plane.

"Afterwards, and usually when the pilots are in their ready room getting out of their togs, the signal officer from his notebook will tell them how they did, or what they didn't do, or what they should have done. All of which can be of help for the next time.

"But the art of signalling planes aboard, and bringing them aboard rapidly with the maximum of safety, is such a complicated art that even when we watch from the island we do not catch the full picture. Or at least we do not catch it in the true perspective. The only place to catch the true perspective actually is right down there next to the signal rack itself.

"From up in the island too, as in the grandstand of any football game, we are tempted each time to be the quarterback. Or in this case, the signal officer. Why doesn't he give the 'wave-off?' Or: Why doesn't he give the 'cut'? Or: Why did he give the 'wave-off?' It looked all right to me.

"Yes, we cannot resist being unofficial signal officers, none of us. All of which adds to the life aboard a carrier, too.

"There's the story which goes how some new captain on one of the smaller carriers had much the same idea about quarterbacking from high up on his distant bridge. Through the loudspeaker the new captain harassed the signal officer so much during the landings, and began yelling to him so much what to do each time, that the signal officer suddenly had to decide between smashing up the planes or his own Navy career. He was so blindly furious about all the dictation during the height of a landing that, using an artist's prerogative (and he certainly was an artist), he tossed his signal paddles onto the deck and went below.

"He aimed for the empty wardroom, and stayed there drinking coffee, trying to drown with it what he was thinking. Meanwhile, the remainder of the planes continued circling and circling the ship waiting for the signals, the pilots wondering what the hell.

"Perhaps the end of the story might have been different if competent landing signal officers were something which could just be picked up for the asking. But months of training, and even years of training, have gone into what they do which may appear so easy. And in addition to their training they also have to have that little 'something else' besides to be classed in the limited group of the truly top-notchers. Their fame, though not known to the public, is certainly known from carrier to carrier in the Pacific.

"A top-notcher, though he may classify himself as 'just another one of those plane-bouncers' is really a gifted personage. It is taken for granted that he can signal the planes on in 'along the groove,' that with his paddles he can talk with the pilots continually, that he can tell them they are too low or too high or at too much of an angle or too fast or too slow. It is taken for granted, also, that he is responsible for making sure their wheels and their flaps are down before they come in. All this part of his ordinary work is understood.

"But a true top-notcher is one who can go beyond any of this. He is the one who knows the personal characteristics of the individual flyers aboard. Some of these flyers, he realizes, are better at one type of approach than another, and some are just naturally so good at carrier-landings that he need not worry too much about them, but can concentrate on the others instead.

"If there is to be uniformity in the landings, naturally, it is well for him to see to it that all the flyers behave more or less the same way. But in those cases of emergency, in those cases where planes have to be brought aboard regardless, and brought aboard fast—these are the moments when the artistry of a signal officer really shows, and really pays dividends.

"He knows in a second what allowances to make for one flyer, and what not to allow for another. Some can get by, and skilfully, with something which might cause others to hit the deck too hard. He will recognize the pilot by the number of his plane, or he may recognize the pilot himself as he circles by. And when a plane has signalled the instant need of an emergency landing regardless of anybody or anything, but preferably a landing on deck, all this depends too on the signal officer's ability. Or when they come in with their big bomb loads still stuck to the plane and unreleasable. Or when they come in with their landing-gear shot away. Or when they come in wounded and bearly able to make it. These are the moments when a true top-notcher, working his most delicate best with the pilot, is surely an artist supreme.

"Anyhow, to return to that story which was started some while back, it was not long before that new captain on the little carrier began imitating the pilots aloft by also wondering what the hell.

"There was no other landing signal officer aboard, so now you know how the story ends. He was summoned from his coffee back up to the flight deck. Nobody coached him over the loudspeaker after that. Nor, according to our version of the story as told to us, did anybody mention court-martial.

"For a landing signal officer is at his best when, along with knowing the rest of his trade, he has the absolute confidence of his flyers—and this one had it. They stuck by him the same as he in turn had stuck by them by not heeding distant advice. If the confidence in a landing signal officer ever has cause to become the least bit wobbly, a pilot consciously or subconsciously may hesitate about the signals at a critically wrong time.

"So all in all a landing signal officer, in his yellow sweater and yellow cloth helmet, may look gaudy out there next to the fantail, and he may look funny waving those colored paddles around his head. But above him there may be as many as sixty pilots and their gunners who would like very much to be able to eat that night. He wants to see to it that they are able."

Bob Croman was an SBD Dauntless dive-bomber pilot in the South Pacific during the Second World War. He was ordered back to the States in March 1944 to attend Landing Signal Officer school and after graduating he was assigned to Carrier Air Group 19, the first U.S. Navy unit to fly the hot new Grumman F8F Bearcat fighter.

Heavy fog had suddenly formed over the Navy airfield at Santa Rosa, California, on 18 July 1945, and the visibility there was less than a half mile. Bob Croman was the LSO for CAG 19 and the unit was practicing field carrier landings for the first time in their new Bearcats. They were quickly discovering that the aeroplane was extremely powerful and wholly unforgiving. Croman was in his position at the end of the runway and with him were an assistant LSO, an ambulance and its crew.

The impressive Bearcat, with its big Pratt & Whitney engine, and huge propeller, developed a lot of torque; its pilot had to 'keep ahead' of the machine or it would get away from him.

The first three planes did well and Croman gave them each a 'cut' signal to land. The next pilot was clearly losing control of his plane in the approach and coming in too slowly. The LSO gave him the 'slow' signal, but the Bearcat continued lower and slower in the approach. At that point, Croman tried desperately to get the errant pilot back on track as the fighter roared towards him. The pilot added power . . . too late. Torque pulled the plane to the left, towards where the LSO stood. It hit the runway hard, collapsing the left wing and landing gear, and twisting the big propeller.

Had this happened aboard a carrier, Bob Croman might have been able to throw himself into the safety net adjacent to the LSO platform, but on this airfield there was no escape for him. Screeching towards him, the Bearcat slid and he dove at the area beneath the plane's right wing and felt a heavy thud. He was lying on his stomach, dazed and unable to move. It seemed to him that he had lain there a very long time. After hitting him, the wrecked Bearcat had continued sliding down the runway, finally coming to a stop. The pilot got out of it without a scratch.

Bob Croman had been flung like a ragdoll by the impact of the plane. He lay on the ground, contorted, his right leg mangled and bleeding profusely. He needed urgent treatment and the other people at the scene rushed to help him. One of them applied a tourniquet and removed Bob's jacket. An ambulance crew medic quickly gave the LSO a shot of morphine. Until then he had felt almost no pain. The the pain arrived. It was nearly unbearable. But with it, he knew he was not dead. You can't hurt that bad and be dead, he thought. At Santa Rosa base dispensary, the doctors could stabilize Croman, whose leg had almost been severed about six inches up from the ankle, and was only still attached by bits of flesh. He was soon flown to the Oakland Naval Hospital and rushed to an operating room.

LSOs at work on the U.S. carrier *Coral Sea*.

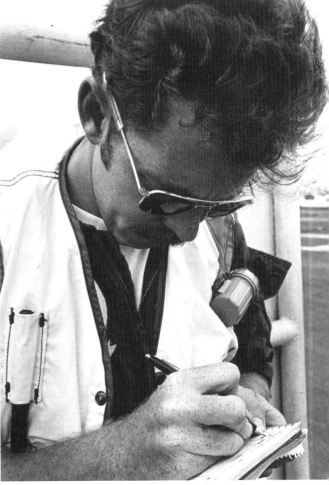

There he was met by a Dr McRae whom he had known briefly fifteen months earlier in the South Pacific. The doctor reattached Croman's leg in an eight-hour surgical procedure.

Over the next five years, Bob Croman underwent sixteen additional operations on his damaged leg. His Navy and flying careers had ended with the tragic accident and he never had more than partial use of his ankle and foot, but was forever grateful to the Navy for the treatment he received and to Dr McRae who had been there for him.

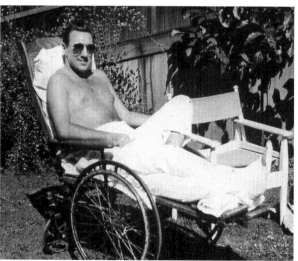

Upper left: The Bell Boeing V-22 Osprey tilt-rotor multi-role vertical take-off and landing aircraft; above: Royal Navy Sea King helicopters aboard a carrier at sea; left: Former SBD dive-bomber pilot Robert Croman, a WW2 landing signal officer, whose right leg was nearly severed when a Bearcat fighter on a landing approach at a Navy airfield near Santa Rosa, California in July 1945, crash-landed striking Croman, who survived thanks to a skilled surgeon at the Oakland Naval Hospital.

Turkey Shoot

In the Pacific theater of the Second World War, much of the main action of the Imperial Japanese Navy was planned around and led by her fleet aircraft carriers. With the Battle of the Philippine Sea, Japan's capability for launching and conducting effective large-scale carrier actions was virtually eliminated. It was the fifth battle between the principal carriers of the IJN and the U.S. Navy and, in addition to carrier-based aircraft, it involved other warships of both nations as well as land-based Japanese aircraft. In it, the Japanese Navy would ultimately lose the great majority of its carrier air strength.

The Japanese military had intended from the beginning of U.S. involvement in the Pacific war to do all they could to cause the Americans to suffer such extreme losses in manpower, equipment, aircraft and warships as to destroy the resolve of the American people and make them weary of the war, to weaken the U.S. militarily and in so doing open the door for Japan to continue her aggressive conquests in eastern and southeast Asia.

In spite of the growing disadvantages experienced by the Japanese as the war progressed, the High Command continued to believe that the Imperial Japanese Navy could fight the U.S. Navy in a single great decisive engagement in which they would defeat the Americans. But with the continuing excessive losses they were experiencing in the carrier battles of the Coral Sea, Midway, and in the Solomon Islands campaign, their capability to fight and win such an action was diminishing. The IJN simply could no longer project the level of force they had previously shown with their carriers. They were unable to replace the losses they were incurring among their skilled carrier pilots.

Still, the Japanese military planners aimed to conduct that decisive engagement with the U.S. Pacific Fleet sometime in early 1944. It would be delayed, however, as the IJN worked to reconstitute its carrier air groups in preparation for the big battle to come. By mid-1943, the navies of the United States and Britain had essentially neutralized the Japanese numerical and technological superiority of the early war years and had overtaken her in the quality and capability of many types of warships and aircraft. The quality of training in virtually all areas of the Allied navies was also superior by this time to that of the IJN.

Admiral Isoroku Yamamoto, among the best and brightest of Japan's military minds and the mastermind and main planner of the Pearl Harbor strike on the American battleship fleet, which brought the U.S. into the war, was killed on 18 April 1943. During an inspection tour of Japanese forward positions in the Solomon Islands, the Mitsubishi Betty bomber in which the admiral was traveling was located and shot down by U.S. Army Air Force P-38 Lightning fighters of the 339th Fighter Squadron. Yamamoto was succeeded by Admiral Mineichi Koga as Commander in Chief of the Japanese Mobile Fleet.

The U.S. Navy Fast Carrier Task Force at that time had taken on a series of missions designed to weaken the Japanese land-based airpower capability and with it, Japan's ability to cope with the coming Allied amphibious invasions of the island-hopping campaign. The missions were so effective, they substantially changed Allied campaign tactics in the remainder of the war.

In their defensive planning, Japanese military commanders considered the Marianas Islands in the

Saipan, Guam, and Tinian, all of which would be vitally important in the American prosecution of the Pacific war. Tinian, in fact, would provide the massive air base from which most of the B-29 fire-bombing raids were flown near the end of the war, as well as the missions of *Enola Gay* and *Bock's Car*, the bombers that delivered the atomic bombs on Hiroshima and Nagasaki in August 1945. But in 1943, the airfields of these islands based Japanese fighters and bombers whose role was the protection of the Japanese home islands and the sea lanes to them.

By early 1944 the powerful U.S. Pacific fleet had breeched Japan's outer defensive circle, through the Marshall Islands and across the central Pacific towards the Marianas. The Japanese Imperial Staff now anticipated that the attentions of the U.S. fleet would next be directed at the Marianas, and that should the U.S. achieve control of the those islands, the big air bases there would put their B-29s within effective range of Japan's home islands. It was that threat to the Marianas that triggered the Japanese decision to go ahead with their long-delayed decisive battle with the American navy.

The U.S. fleet's Fast Carrier Task Force in 1944 was known as Task Force 58 and was commanded by Admiral Marc Mitscher. It was the primary fighting unit of the Navy and as such was the prime target of the Japanese in their battle plan. Though they were outnumbered in warships and aircraft, they

Alex Vraciu was the fourth highest-scoring U.S. Navy fighter ace of the Second World War.

would augment their carrier-based air power with substantial land-based aircraft. The greater range of these land-based aircraft enabled them to engage the U.S. carriers. And they intended to launch land-based aircraft from their island bases in the area, send them to attack the U.S. carriers and then land on other Japanese-occupied island airfields. They would then shuttle back to the original island bases, attacking the U.S. fleet again on the return flight. The Japanese planners knew too, that carrier-based aircraft (of any navy) required a head wind blowing down the flight deck to enable the aircraft to launch, and that the Central Pacific was dominated by easterly trade winds. Thus, the carriers of the U.S. fleet would have to be steaming eastward to launch and recover their aircraft. Positioning the Japanese fleet to the west of the Marianas then would ideally place it to both initiate and break off the battle, giving themselves the key initiative in the situation.

It began on 12 June when aircraft from the American carriers flew a series of air attacks against the Marianas, which persuaded the Japanese commanders that the U.S. was about to invade the islands. It also surprised many of them who had been convinced that the next major move by the enemy forces would be more to the south, probably on the Palaus or the Carolines. In that belief, they had stationed a minimal force of just fifty aircraft to protect the Marianas. On 13 June, warships of the U.S. fleet began bombarding Saipan in preparation for invading it. The action caused the Japanese fleet commander to order a counterattack which was to be mounted by six Japanese carriers, and a number of battleships, all of them set to rendezvous on 16 June in the western Philippine Sea, where they would be refueled.

On 15 June seamen aboard U.S. Navy submarines sighted warships of the Japanese fleet. This enemy force consisted of the carriers *Hiyo, Junyo, Shokaku, Taiho*, and *Zuikaku*, the four light carriers *Chitose, Chiyoda, Ryuho*, and *Zuiho*, the five battleships *Haruna, Kongo, Musashi, Nagato*, and *Yamato*, together with their support cruisers, destroyers, and oilers. By the afternoon of the 18th, Admiral Mitscher had Task Force 58 formed up near Saipan ready to engage the Japanese fleet. The element of the task force nearest the enemy fleet was made up of the seven fast battleships *Alabama, Indiana, Iowa, New Jersey, North Carolina, South Dakota*, and *Washington*. Additionally, in support of the entire task force were eight heavy cruisers, thirteen light cruisers, fifty-eight destroyers and twenty-eight submarines. The various aircraft carriers present were organized into three groups of four. The first carrier group contained the *Bataan, Belleau Wood, Hornet*, and *Yorktown*. The second group contained the *Bunker Hill, Cabot, Monterey*, and *Wasp*, and the last group was composed of the *Enterprise, Lexington, Princeton*, and *San Jacinto*. In addition to these, there was a further group of three carriers including the *Cowpens, Essex*, and *Langley*.

By 05.50 in the morning of 19 June, one of the Japanese Zero aircraft stationed on Guam had flown a search patrol and the pilot had sighted the American Task Force 58. He radioed his report of the sighting and then dove to attack one of the U.S. destroyers on the fringe of the task force. He was quickly shot down.

Moments later, radar contacts by U.S. warships in the area began establishing the locations of various Japanese naval forces and a squadron of F6F Hellcat fighters was launched from the carrier *Belleau Wood* to patrol the area around Orote airfield, Guam, where many Japanese aircraft were taking off. In the ensuing air battle, thirty-five Japanese aircraft were downed. Most of the Hellcats returned safely to the carrier.

above: The powerful Grumman Hellcat fighter proved its worth hundreds of times in the Pacific theatre of World War Two. The 19 June 1944 air battle known as the 'Great Marianas Turkey Shoot' showcased the Hellcat's performance. The Japanese Navy was no longer a significant threat to Allied forces in the western Pacific after the battle.

Radars of several TF58 vessels had picked up enemy warship contacts 150 miles to the west by 10 a.m., as well as a force of sixty-eight enemy aircraft in the first Japanese carrier-based raid of the battle. All available TF58 aircraft were launched and, in the resulting clash, twenty-five Japanese planes were shot down, for the loss of one Hellcat. Other groups of U.S. fighters soon arrived and took part in the action, downing a further sixteen enemy aircraft. Only three Japanese bombers managed to get through the U.S. fighters and attack the battleships of TF58, one of them getting a direct hit on the *South Dakota* causing several casualties, but the battleship was able to carry on in the action. None of the Japanese aircraft was able to get through to hit the American carriers. In five hours of attacks by Japanese aircraft, 143 of their own aircraft were shot down.

On the morning of 19 June 1944, Lieutenant J.G. Alex Vraciu (rhymes with cashew) and his squadron of twelve aircraft were launched to supplement the *Lexington* combat air patrol which was already airborne. Radar had picked up a force of bogies approaching the U.S. fleet in several large groups. Vraciu was leading the second of three four-plane divisions. As the Hellcats climbed at full military power, he heard the Lex fighter director (FDO) radio: "Vector 250. Climb to 25,000 pronto!" The protracted climb at full power was proving too much for some of the Hellcats. Vraciu's engine began to throw a film of oil over his windshield, forcing him to ease back slightly on the throttle. However, his division stayed together and two additional Hellcats joined up with them. All were struggling in the climb and soon accepted that the maximum height they would attain that day was 20,000 feet, a fact they duly reported to the FDO. On the way up to their ceiling altitude, Vraciu noticed his wingman, Brockmeyer, repeatedly pointing towards Alex's wing. He didn't know what Brockmeyer was trying to communicate until much later when he learned that his wings (which folded to take up less space on board the carrier) were not fully locked. The red safety barrel locks were showing.

The aerial engagement that Vraciu's group was heading for was over before they reached the enemy planes. His group was ordered to come back and orbit at 20,000 feet over the task force. When they arrived over the American ships, the FDO directed the Hellcats to a new heading of 265°. There were bogies about seventy-five miles out. On the way to the intercept, Vraciu's group saw seven more Hellcats converging from the starboard side.

After flying about twenty-five miles Alex spotted three bogies and began to close on them. He guessed that there were probably more enemy aircraft in the area and soon saw what he estimated to be at least fifty planes 2,000 feet below the Hellcats and on their port side. He was excited and was thinking that the situation could easily develop into a fighter pilot's dream. There did not seem to be any top cover escort with the bogies which, by this time, were identifiable as Japanese aircraft. He picked out the nearest inboard straggler, a Judy dive-bomber, and started a run on it.

Alex peripherally sensed the presence of another Hellcat which seemed to be intent upon the same enemy aircraft that he was after. Concerned about the possibility of being blind-sided by the other American, he chose to abort his run, roaring under the Japanese formation and taking the opportunity to quickly look them over. He noted that there were Judys, Jills, and Zeros, pulled up and over the enemy assemblage and selected another Judy out on the edge of the formation. The enemy plane was doing a bit of manoeuvring as Vraciu approached it from behind. The Japanese rear gunner was firing at him as he closed in. He returned fire and the Judy erupted in flame and began to trail a long smoke plume down to the sea.

Pulling back up to the enemy formation, Alex found two more Judys on the loose, came in from

left: Carrier pilots await a briefing in their ready room; bottom left: WW2 fighter ace Stanley Vejtasa who later was captain of the carrier USS *Constellation*; below: Second World War naval aviators Edward O'Hare and James Thach; right: Grumman F6F Hellcats on the flight deck of the carrier USS *Yorktown* in 1943; below right: A Curtiss SB2C Helldiver dive-bomber being spotted for take-off from an *Essex* class carrier in WW2.

A Grumman F6F Hellcat beginning its take-off roll.

their rear and fired, sending one down in flames. Still on the same pass, he slipped the Hellcat into position behind the other Judy and just as quickly sent it down, its rear gunner continuing to fire at him as the enemy plane fell. Three down

The great mass of turning, twisting U.S. and Japanese aircraft was moving ever closer to the American fleet. By this time the Japanese formation was badly broken up, but many of its aircraft remained on course towards the U.S. ships. Vraciu reported this fact to his carrier. Then another enemy plane broke formation in his view and he slid over into position after it. He had to be quite careful now and get in very close as his windshield had become increasingly oil-smeared and difficult to see through. A single short burst proved sufficient to set the enemy plane alight and cause it to enter a wildly out-of-control spin.

The air battle was now much closer to the U.S. ships, and the Jills started descending into their torpedo runs. The remaining Judys were just about to peel off on their bombing runs. Alex saw a group of three Judys in trail and headed for the tail-ender. At this point he and they were almost over the outer destroyer screen, but still fairly high. Alex noticed a black puff of flak in the sky near him and realized that the American five-inch guns were firing at the enemy aircraft in defence of the U.S. fleet. He overtook the nearest Judy, fired the briefest of bursts and saw the plane's engine come apart in pieces. It alternately smoked and burned as it disappeared below.

Now Alex spotted another enemy aircraft, this one just into its diving attack on an American destroyer. He caught up with the plane and was amazed when yet another very short burst from his Hellcat's guns caused the Japanese to explode, seemingly right in his face. He guessed that his bullets must have hit the enemy's bomb. He had seen planes blow up before, but never like that. He was forced to manoeuver wildly to avoid the hot, scattering debris of the kill.

As he recovered and climbed back up to rejoin some of the other Hellcats, Vraciu observed that the sky was now entirely free of enemy aircraft. He noticed too, that a thirty-five-mile-long pattern of flaming oil slicks lay on the water behind them. He later discovered that, owing to his oil-smeared windshield and the need to work in really close to the enemy planes, he had actually fired only 360 rounds of ammunition in shooting down six Judy's, all in less than eight minutes.

The next day, 20 June, while flying escort for bomber and torpedo planes in the record 300-mile strike against the Japanese fleet on the second day of the First Battle of the Philippine Sea, Alex Vraciu shot down a Zero, his nineteenth and final victory. For his achievements between 12 and 20 June 1944, he was awarded the Navy Cross.

On 20 June the pilots and radiomen of VB-10 were hoping that the Japanese fleet would be found before the end of the day. At 4.30 p.m. their ready room was alerted that the enemy fleet had indeed been located roughly 250 miles away. Jack Glass, an SBD gunner, USS *Enterprise*: "We were very worried about such a long mission so late in the day. If we somehow made it back to our carriers, it would mean night landings. All of our pilots were qualified for night landings, but had made only a few. I knew this would probably be the last crack at the Jap fleet before the invasion of Japan.

"The flight to the Japanese fleet took about two hours. The time was spent checking out our guns, looking for enemy fighters, and operating our radar, hoping to pick up our target. My pilot, Lieutenant Oliver W. Hubbard, was leading the second section in skipper 'Jig Dog' Ramage's division. Lt. Bangs was leading the other division. Hubbard had agreed that a hit was a must. The skipper sent Bangs and his division to one carrier, and our division took the *Ryuho*. The anti-aircraft fire was very strong but we managed to get into our dive with no problem, with the exception of a half-hearted attack by several Zeros which were promptly taken care of by our fighters. In our dive we became twisted around trying to get on target. We had to settle for a port-to-starboard run and only scored a near miss. On our pull-out, we were headed away from our return heading and had to do a 180 back through the entire fleet, skipping over ship after ship. The battleships were firing their main batteries as we went by. I was strafing everything in sight, mainly out of frustration.

"After leaving the fleet, our main thought was finding our way back to our task force. Again, it was about a two-hour flight. Our new radar worked fine and we picked up the *Enterprise* at about 100 miles. There were many frantic calls about fuel problems and going in the drink, but the old faithful

SBDs just kept chugging along. As I recall, Jig Dog made only one transmission . . . 'Land on any base.' We did just that, finding the *Wasp* right away. We had barely left the plane and entered the island hatch when a Hellcat crashed the barrier, putting the *Wasp* out of operation for about twenty-five minutes. The next morning I measured our fuel. We had less than three gallons remaining. Without the excellent landing by Lt. Hubbard, we would have taken a swim that night. A flight of over five and a half hours in a plane that wasn't supposed to fly more than about four hours. That's fuel management."

In nearly every respect, the American forces went into the action with a significant edge over the opposition. In tactics and technology, in pilot and crew training and anti-aircraft gunnery, in aircraft and warship design, construction and performance, by June 1944 the Japanese were outmatched. In sheer strength of numbers the Americans went into the battle with seven fleet aircraft carriers, eight light fleet carriers, seven battleships, seventy-nine additional warships, twenty-eight submarines, and more than 950 aircraft. The Japanese fielded five fleet carriers, four light carriers, five battleships, nineteen additional warships, twenty-four submarines, 450 carrier-based aircraft and 300 land-based aircraft. By the end of the action, U.S. losses amounted to one battleship damaged and 123 aircraft destroyed. The Japanese lost three fleet carriers, two oilers, and between 550 and 650 aircraft destroyed. So lopsided were the results of the aerial action that one American pilot from the carrier *Lexington* memorably remarked: "This is like an old-time turkey shoot!"

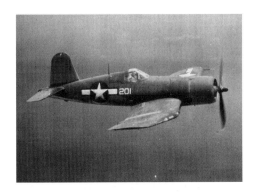

far left: Once told by his Navy flying instructor, "You will never solo. You are the dumbest cadet I have ever laid eyes on," U.S. Marine night-fighter ace Bruce Porter became one of the great fighter pilots of the Second World War; left: A Vought F4U Corsair out of Guadalcanal in 1944; top right: Grumman Avenger ready for takeoff; bottom left and right: views of the Grumman F6F Hellcat.

The workload on the flight deck of today's aircraft carrier has evolved from the jobs and requirements of the fast attack carriers of World War Two. Aircraft, equipment, and technologies have certainly changed over the years, but the fundamental role of bringing an Air Wing, its personnel and aircraft, to wherever it is needed in the world, and operating naval aviation there, is still the priority.

Shirt colour differentiation is how to tell who does which jobs on the flight deck of a modern U.S. Navy aircraft carrier. In today's U.S. Navy, the men—and increasingly, the women—are identifiable by the jerseys they wear. On the American carriers the tractor drivers, aeroplane handlers, aircraft elevator operators, and the phone talkers and messengers wear blue jerseys. Brown shirts are for Air Wing plane captains and leading Petty Officers, while the Air Wing maintenance people, catapult and arresting gear crews, quality assurance personnel, cargo handlers, hook-runners, ground support equipment trouble-shooters, helicopter landing signal enlisted personnel, and ship's photographers all wear Green. Purple is the shade worn by aviation fuel personnel; and ordnance, crash, salvage, and explosive ordnance personnel all wear Red. Squadron plane inspectors, landing signal officers, air transfer officers, liquid oxygen crews, safety observers, and medical personnel all wear White. Yellow jerseys denote aircraft handling officers, plane directors, and catapult and arresting gear officers.

British Royal Navy flight deck personnel on its active modern carriers wore a coloured vest known as a surcoat which, as with the their American navy counterparts, identified them by function. In the RN, Flight Deck Officers, the Chief of the Flight Deck, and aircraft directors wore Yellow surcoats, while Blue surcoats were reserved for naval airmen and photographers. Brown surcoats denoted aircraft and engine full supervisory ratings, and Air electrical full supervisory ratings wore Green. Air radio full supervisory ratings wore Green with a Blue stripe. Red surcoats were the identifier of the crash and salvage parties. Weapon supply/all ratings wore Red with a Black Stripe. Flight deck assault guides wore Red with a White stripe. Medical attendants wore White with a Red cross. Deck supervisors, duty aircrew, watch chiefs, and Air Engineering Officers wore White. Flight deck engineers wore White with a Black stripe, and aircraft engine mechanics wore Grey.

Preparation for flight operations aboard an aircraft carrier of the U.S. Navy actually begin the day before the ops are scheduled. In the evening before, an Air Plan is prepared outlining the entire scheduled activity of the operation. The plan is distributed the night before and includes all information required for all concerned. It includes the information about the mission itself: the number of sorties to be flown, the fuel and ordnance load requirements, and the tactical communication frequencies to be used, as well as the launch and recovery times. The flight quarters are announced and manned. No crew members who are not directly involved in flight operations are allowed to be on the flight deck or in the deck-edge catwalks.

The briefing for the pilots and aircrew is given on the specifics of their mission and the sequence of events planned. They are due at their aircraft thirty to forty-five minutes before they are scheduled to launch, giving them ample time to complete a thorough pre-flight inspection of their aircraft before the order to start engines.

While all the above is going on, the various flight deck personnel are readying their gear and equipment for the upcoming op. Well before any aircraft engines are started, the ritual foreign object damage (FOD) walk-down is conducted in which all off-duty personnel, mainly Air Wing and flight deck,

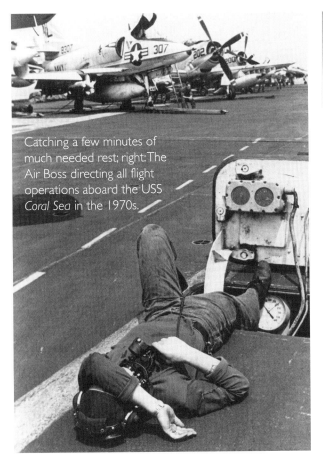

Catching a few minutes of much needed rest; right: The Air Boss directing all flight operations aboard the USS *Coral Sea* in the 1970s.

participate. Normally, the walk-down is sponsored by one of the Air Wing squadrons and lively music is provided for their motivation. With the gamut of aircraft maintenance and repair occurring on the flight deck, it is virtually inevitable that small items such as rivets, bits of safety wire, and small tools hit the deck during such activity and are not noticed at the time. Later, when the aircraft engines are running, such objects can be blown around and cause potential injury to people and damage to engines. Tiny objects can sometimes be found hidden in the recessed 'pad-eye' aircraft tie-down points that are spotted all over the flight deck. Just ahead of the walk-down force, personnel manning air hoses proceed to blow any collected debris or water from the pad-eyes, before the deck-wide line of FOD-walkers slowly make their way down the entire length of the flight deck, retrieving all objects that may pose even the slightest threat to man and machine. In their wake, stroll a group of personnel pushing scrubber vacuums to remove anything that may have been overlooked by the FOD-walkers. Carrier operations experience has shown foreign object damage to be a deadly menace to personnel, aircraft, and equipment, so the FOD-walk procedure is a serious, no-nonsense preliminary of every carrier flight operation. The start-engines order is never given until the FOD-walk has been completed.

Rotary aircraft are the first machines scheduled to start up and launch in a flight operation; they are the plane guard helicopters which depart to orbit the ship in a D-shaped pattern, so as to be in

left: Deck crew aboard a Royal Navy carrier in the 1940s; below: Second World War U.S. Navy aviators preparing for a mission; right: Helicopter operations on the carrier HMS *Illustrious* in the late 1990s; centre: The SB2C Curtiss Helldiver.

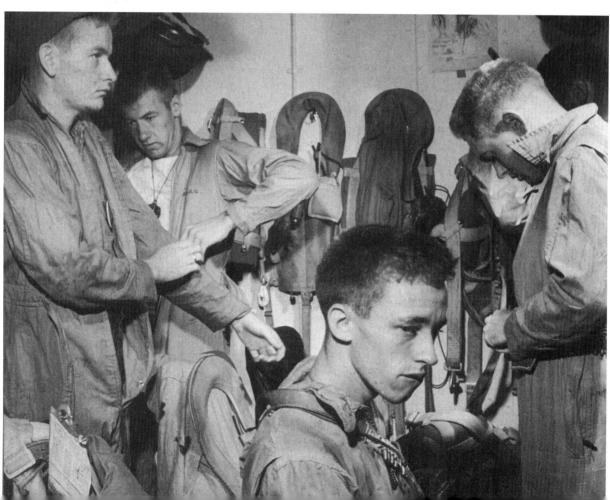

position to quickly rescue an airman or aircrew member in an emergency situation.

When the fixed-wing aircraft scheduled to fly the mission are ready to launch, the giant *Nimitz*-class supercarrier is turned into the wind to pick up the normally required thirty-knots of wind over the flight deck for take-offs. It is then that the yellow-shirted plane directors guide the first aircraft to be launched to precise positions on the two forward steam catapults. As soon as the planes are spotted on those positions, large jet blast deflectors rise from the deck just behind the planes, to protect flight deck personnel just aft of the catapults. Now it's the job of the hook-up greenshirts, who crouch at the nose wheels of the aircraft on cats one and two and attach the nose gear to the catapult shuttle with nose-tow and hold-back bars. Another greenshirt then moves in to the right of one plane's canopy and holds up a black box with illuminated numerals flashing the predicted weight of the air-craft. The pilot must then concur that the figure is correct. That done, the cat launch personnel cali-brate the power of the cat to the requirement of the plane about to launch. Low clouds of steam billow down the length of the cat as a yellowshirt signals the pilot, who releases the brakes and

below and right: HMS *Illustrious* at sea; far right: An EA-IF Spad Skyraider with jammers on the outboard wing stations and a radar pod on the inboard right wing, departs the USS *Constellation*.

applies full power. The cat officer signals with a rotating hand, , two fingers extended, as the pilot does a quick final check that the aircraft and controls are functioning correctly. He then salutes to indicate that he is ready to launch, and braces himself. If he is flying an F/A-18 Hornet, U.S. Navy procedure requires him to place his right or stick hand on the canopy frame grab-handle and keep it there for the duration of the cat shot.

At this point, the catapult officer checks the final readiness of the cat and receives confirmation from other flight deck personnel that the aircraft is ready for flight. He then signals the shooter in the enclosed launch station bubble (by touching the deck) to press the cat firing button. Launch ... and the four G force of the steam cat hurls the aeroplane from the flight deck. The plane reaches 150 knots air speed from a standing start in two seconds, sending the flesh and facial muscles of the pilot racing towards the back of his or her skull.

With the departure of the first two mission aircraft, the catapult crews hurry to position and attach the next planes in the queue for launch. They can ready and launch an aircraft every thirty seconds if necessary. Frequently, they are required to set up and launch aircraft more than one-hundred times in a day. For the flight deck to run smoothly, an endless routine of planning, training, discipline, expert engineering, highly skilled maintenance, motivation, and nearly superhuman attention to detail is required. The primary concern overall is safety.

Airline pilot David Smith, when a naval aviator, accumulated more than 1,000 hours flying the Grumman F-14 Tomcat between 1982 and 1991. During that period, he made 342 carrier traps (landings) over the course of two Mediterranean cruises aboard the USS *John F. Kennedy* (CVA-67). After that, he instructed F-14 and F/A-18 pilots in adversary tactics at Key West, Florida, where all of the F/A-18

above: Grumman TBF Avengers; left: A Fairey Firefly landing accident on a Royal Navy carrier.

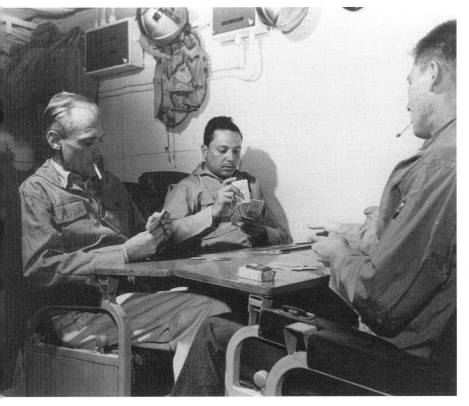

upper left: A famous Royal Navy aviator of the Falklands War, Commander Nigel 'Sharkey' Ward; upper right: Captain Eric 'Winkle' Brown, has flown more aircraft types than any pilot in history; left: Downtime finds these fliers enjoying a relaxing game in their carrier ready room..

pilots who flew in the Gulf War Operation Desert Storm were trained. "We F-14 pilots flew whenever the ship had air operations. In a normal schedule, we flew during the day and every other night. Some of us flew every night, to make up for some of the weak night pilots and the senior squadron officers who just didn't want to fly at night. Flying at night was not fun. Flying in the day was, and everyone wanted to do that.

"Most flight ops lasted either one hour and thirty minutes or one hour and forty-five minutes. In peacetime, the briefs started between one-and-a-half and two-hours before launch. The topics included such admin items as weather, aircraft, crews, join-up (rendezvous), lost communications, gas (inflight refueling amounts, altitudes and locations), and the mission briefing itself, which took longer and varied from ship support, to air-to-air basic fighter manoeuvring, to air intercept, to strafing, to section or division tactics. If operating near land, we might be supporting an overland operation or working with another country. The brief was where you transitioned from just being aboard the ship, to being reminded of why you were there. The actual brief was almost a formality because you had heard it all many times before, but it always served to make me focus on what I was about to do.

"If the brief ran long, you would walk immediately to Maintenance Control to check out the logbook on your airplane. You then signed for the airplane and went to the Paraloft, where flight equipment was stored. On the *Kennedy* it was a small room, no bigger than an average bedroom. With all of the hanging equipment, it could barely accommodate four persons. This was where you became an aviator. You went about the task of suiting up and preparing to go topside to do something that no one else on the planet was going to do at that moment.

"On the flight deck it was usually very quiet and rather peaceful at the beginning of a new ops cycle. Normally, it was a very dangerous place.

"The first task was to find your plane. There was never a clue as to where it would be spotted. You walked around the flight deck until you found the aircraft number you were looking for. People have been known to man the wrong airplane. Finding your airplane at night can be difficult and frustrating. When you found it, the plane captain (who might be just eighteen years old) would exchange a few words with you about the only thing you had in common: that airplane. I knew all my plane captains and all the maintenance personnel very well.

Pre-flighting an F-14 on board a carrier can be the most dangerous part of the mission. Some of them were parked with their tails hanging out over the edge of the ship. There could be twenty to thirty knots of wind over the deck, and trying to do a thorough pre-flight might put you in the safety nets, if not actually overboard. Walking around the plane you encountered chains that were trying to trip you, and many other little gotchas out to ruin your day.

"Climbing in and sitting in the seat of the Tomcat was a relief, a place of comfort. You knew your way around the cockpit with your eyes closed, and you felt safe. Because the F-14 burns gas fast, we always launched right after the E-2 Hawkeye (our eyes and ears) and the A-6 Intruder/tanker (our gas). A couple of F-14s would be spotted either on the catapults or just behind them. When the order was given, engines were started and we went through the various after-start checks.

"We had afterburners, but did not always need them for the cat shot. On deployment, when you are going to launch missiles and have a full load of fuel, you would always be using afterburners in the launch. You followed the plane director's instructions and he would steer you into alignment just behind the catapult. He would then point to another plane director who was straddling the cat track about thirty feet ahead of your plane. He would slowly lead you forward until you were just behind

One of the many U.S. Navy escort carriers that played such a vital part in the Second World War, the USS *Badoeng Strait*, with Vought F4U Corsairs aboard.

the cat shuttle. Another director would guide you very precisely onto the shuttle and you would then be turned over to the CAT officer. When satisfied that your hook-up was correct, he would have the tension taken on your plane. Under tension, you would be required to go to full power. You did not come out of full power under any circumstances unless the CAT officer stepped in front of your plane and gave you the 'throttle back' signal. This was a trust that had been violated in the past, costing lives. Once under tension and in full power, you were going flying.

"During the day you can see all of the actors on the stage. At night you see nothing but the yellow wands. Two totally different worlds. The difference is almost indescribable. "The plane is under tension and at full power and, when the CAT officer is content that all of the check-list items have been checked, he will give the signal to launch by touching the deck. Now the fun begins. F-14 pilots have long been accused of trying to be 'cool' by holding the head well forward during a launch, instead of

Pioneering aviator Eugene Ely with one of the Curtiss Pusher aircraft he flew in early 'aircraft carrier' demonstrations.

of keeping it back against the headrest as most aviators do. Actually, when the launch bar releases, the airplane abruptly squats, it's almost like hitting a pothole in the road. Your head is forced down and forward for a split second. This is quickly followed by an immediate and, hopefully, incredible acceleration forward. The neophyte who puts his or her head back against the headrest at the start of this sequence, will have it jolted forward—and then back—with amazing sharpness that will literally make him or her see stars.

"The intensity of the acceleration can vary, depending on the initial gross weight of the plane and the natural wind over the deck. You need a given end/air speed to go flying, and the heavier your plane is, the greater that air speed has to be. Less wind over the deck requires a harder, more powerful cat shot. At a maximum gross weight of 72,000 pounds, an F-14A, with little or no wind over the deck, requires a cat shot that will take the breath out of you. The acceleration is so rapid, it hurts. Such cat shots are not only hard on the pilot and the RIO [radar intercept officer in the back seat], they are hard on the plane as well. Generators, inertial navigation system alignments, radars . . . all are in jeopardy in such launches. Stories of instruments coming out and striking aircrew in the face and chest are not uncommon.

"On an extremely windy day, when the ship is barely moving, you may become concerned that your launch will not be hard enough to send you flying. That concern is directed towards the CAT officer, who may be about to shoot you into water breaking over the deck. He will try to time the launch with the ship's pitches, but a cat shot into a severe down cycle will give you a windscreen full of ocean that you won't soon forget. Still, when things work, and they most always do, the cat shot is the most enjoyable part of the cycle. Getting back on board is something else."

When the flight deck is clear and no operations are scheduled, ship's personnel are often permitted to exercise there and run laps around the immense 1,100-foot-long flight deck.

When the Royal Navy was operating Sea Harrier vertical take-off and landing jets from HMS *Illustrious* in the 1990s, Leading Aircraftman/Aircraft Handler Chris Hurst was aboard and involved in the flight operations activity: "Ten minutes prior to launch, we'd get a verbal communication from the flight control position to start the aircraft. Permission would then be given to the aircraft mechanics to liase with the pilots to start the engines and go through their various acceleration checks, making sure the wing flaps, etc, are at the right angles for launch, depending on the aircraft weights and weapon loads. The mechanics would also take off the outrigger ground locks and the lashings that are not required. Then they would be ready on deck.

"The aircraft directors would face towards the flying control position, watching for an amber light which meant that the ship was on a designated flying course and we had permission to taxi the aircraft onto the runway. The pilot would be told to 'un-brakes.' The two remaining nose lashings and the chocks would be removed. Then a Leading Aircraftman would guide the aircraft out of the range and pass it on to the Petty Officer of the Deck who was standing on the runway at the designated launch distance. He would then marshal it onto that launch distance, stop it on the brakes and pass the control of the aircraft launch to either the Captain of the flight deck, or the Flight Deck Officer, whichever was on watch at the time.

"The duty squadron Air Engineering Officer would then look round the aircraft and make sure everything was safe, all the relevent pins had been removed, etc. When he was satisfied, he would give a thumbs-up to the Flight Deck Officer, who would wait for a steady green light from Flyco, which meant he had the Captain's permission to launch fixed-wing aircraft.

"Then, when he had checked up and down the runway that all was clear, he would raise a small green flag. The pilot would turn on a white nose wheel light and roar away up the deck and off the ski-ramp. As that aircraft was launched the next aircraft would be drawn out of the range and marshalled on in sequence, until all the aircraft had gone.

"All the time this was going on, there was a spare aircraft handling team ready in 'the graveyard' at the front of the deck, should anything go wrong. We called it the graveyard because it was for dead aircraft. They had a tractor ready to attach to the aircraft. Certain minor unserviceabilities could mean an aircraft not launching but having to taxi all the way up to the graveyard to get it out of the way, to clear the deck and make everything ready for the next aircraft to launch. There was nothing worse

above: The Grumman TBF Avenger torpedo bomber approaching to land aboard this U.S. carrier; left: A wounded U.S. Navy gunner is helped from the turret of his TBF; below: A Bell Boeing V-22 Osprey vertical take-off and landing multi-mission aircraft which went operational in the U.S. Marine Corps in 2007.

than an aircraft having a minor radio problem, sitting there with all its intake blanks missing. It was dangerous. Foreign object damage could occur with an aircraft zooming up the deck, so we preferred to get him straight to the graveyard and out of the way."

Former U.S. Navy pilot Jack Kleiss: "The *Enterprise* flight deck was 109 feet abeam (including the island) and approximately 800 feet long. Usually less than half of that length was available for Scouting Six, because the TBDs of Torpedo Six and the SBDs of Bombing Six were always in the pack behind us. "We frequently watched a bomb-laden SBD drop out of sight as it took off and passed the bow of the ship. It then reappeared, picking up speed, getting a boost from the sixty-five-foot deck height and the 'ground effect' between wings and water.

"One day I was up on deck watching as a young pilot really almost touched the waves ahead of the ship. He later confided that he had taken off with his controls fully locked. Somehow he managed to remove the unlocking pin under the control stick, barely avoiding a crash into the sea. He must have been a contortionist."

And another recollection from Kleiss: "One afternoon while Ensign Willie West and I were walking and talking to each other on the flight deck of the *Enterprise*, neither of us heard the centerline elevator warning signal—if it was sounded. Suddenly, Willie took a step into space, and I was right on the edge of the gaping hole.

"I expected to find him in a crumpled heap at the end of a thirty-foot drop. Instead, he walked away unhurt. He said that the elevator was moving downward almost as fast as he was falling, and that jumping on it was like landing on a feather bed."

M. S. Cochran was assigned to the USS *Enterprise* in the Second World War: "We had just left Majuro anchorage. We were on our way to Hollandia. Due to strike there on 21 April. We were getting close to Hollandia, in an area where strict security required a darkened ship. AOM2/c Petty had left the fighter armory with AOM1/c F.S. Rice, heading towards the port bow. It was one of those nights when you literally could not see your hand in front of your face. Both men were cautious and felt somewhat safe because they thought the 'safety chain' was up across the bow. Neither realized that we had spotted two F4U night fighters at 'ready' on the catapults, with the pilots in them prepared for instant take-off. The safety chain was down.

"Petty was a step or two in front of Rice when suddenly Rice heard a muffled grunt. It didn't take him long to realize that Petty had walked off the bow. Rice immediately ran aft to the LSO's platform where he grabbed some float lights, and without thinking of the consequences, threw some of them overboard. What a sight to suddenly see lights behind the ship in that total darkness. Alert men on watch were quick to report. General Quarters was sounded and this particular GQ caught everyone at a time when 'tense' didn't begin to describe how jumpy we were.

"The Officer of the Deck sounded 'man overboard' and every division met for immediate muster and roll call. Destroyers guarding the rear of the Task Force were given the OK to search for Petty. They directed their efforts to the float lights, but there was only one thing wrong with that. The length of flight deck that Rice had to travel to get to the LSO platform would take a fast runner forty to fifty seconds. The ship was moving at a fair rate of speed. In the time he took to run that distance, the closest light to Petty was judged to be a half mile away. The seas were also running choppy at four feet.

The odds of finding Petty were in the needle-in-a-haystack category. We were thinking we would never see Petty again.

"However, there are survivors, some of which are extremely lucky, and some personally self-sufficient. Petty was both. The whale boats which the destroyers sent to look for him did an ever-expanding circle search out from the float lights. They had just decided to halt the search when they heard Petty whistle. He could not see them, but he heard their voices, so he managed to whistle with his fingers to his teeth. That is what saved him. He also helped himself by tying knots in his dungarees and filling them full of air as a float.

"We were back at Pearl in January 1944. Petty had gone on liberty and come back with tattoos of a rooster on one foot and a pig on the other. Old seamen's lore has it that a sailor who does that will never drown. When we next returned to Pearl in July, we had sailors by the dozen getting tattooed with pigs and roosters on their insteps."

left: This F/A-18 Hornet multi-role fighter survived a mid-air collision with another Hornet and returned safely to NAS Oceana, Virginia, in 1996. In the accident, the plane lost its radome, radar, canopy, an access door, and a centreline fuel tank. It also sustained foreign object damage to its starboard engine; right: The kamikaze pilots were members of special attack units near the end of the Second World War. Their mission was to be human bombs, one with their aeroplanes, sacrificing themselves by diving their planes into enemy ships with the goal of sinking them.

In the legendary Mitsubishi A6M Zero fighter, the naval aviator Saburo Sakai was credited with downing sixty-four Allied aircraft during the Second World War. In the first years of the war, the Zero was among the best fighter planes in the world, with its superior manoeuvrability, range and performance. Saburo Sakai, is among the most famous, and certainly among the greatest of the Japanese fighter pilots in that war. He served in the Imperial Japanese Navy and, for most of his flying career, was associated with the Zero fighter in its various models. At least 1,500 of his 3,700 hours of flying time was in Zeros.

When the Second World War began in the Pacific, the Zero fighter was unquestionably superior to virtually all other fighter planes in the world. Of all its potential adversaries in the air, the best American example at the time was probably the Curtiss P-40, which objectively was not quite in the same class with the Japanese fighter, except when in the hands of the best American pilots whose skills and capability helped it overcome the imbalance. Certainly, the others, the Brewster Buffalo—obsolete and far less capable; and the Bell P-39 Airacobra—even with its big cannon, were not much competition for the Zero. Among naval aircraft, the main opponent the Zero faced in the early part of the war was the American Grumman F4F Wildcat, whose manoeuvrability may have been a bit better when being handled by U.S. Navy aviators of at least equal competence to that of the opposition. The fine British Spitfire and Hurricane, as effective as they had been in the Battle of Britain, proved much less so when they encountered the Japanese fighter in 1942.

The Zero was the primary mount of most of Japan's highest achieving fighter aces, including—in order of their number of victories—Hiroyoshi Nishizawa, Shoichi Sugita, Tadashi Nakajima, Saburo Sakai, Naoishi Kanno, Teimei Akamatsu, and Kinsuke Muto.

One factor making the Zero special was its extraordinary range of more than 1,265 miles (1,930 miles with drop tanks). The range made it the only fighter capable, as early as 1938, of escorting bombers all the way to their extremely distant targets and back, until the advent of the American P-51 Mustang in late 1943.

Among the secrets of the Zero's success in those early days was the approach taken by her designer, Jiro Horikoshi, who was charged with meeting the requirements of the Imperial Japanese Navy for the new plane: fast climb, high speed, great range, and superior manoeuvrability. To achieve those characteristics, Horikoshi opted for very low wing-loading, no armour protection for the pilot, and no self-sealing fuel tanks.

On the downside, while the Zero fighter excelled at low and medium altitudes, enabling its pilots to outfight any Allied fighter on most occasions, its performance degraded at high altitudes in the early war years.

The A6M2 version of the Mitsubishi plane, the first production Zero, which the Japanese used in the Pearl Harbor attack on 7 December 1941, was powered by a fourteen-cylinder Nakajima Sakae air-cooled engine developing 950 hp at 13,800 feet. The Model 21 version was designed with folding wingtips for operations from Japan's aircraft carriers. The A6M2 was capable of 316 mph at 16,400 feet. It was armed with two 7.7mm machine-guns and two 20mm cannon.

As the war continued, advanced versions of the Zero were introduced, with the A6M5a production model featuring improved cannon armament, and a top speed of 360 mph. The next model, the A6M5b, finally had an armoured-glass windscreen, automatic fire extinguishers for the fuel tanks, further improved cannon armament, all increasing the plane's weight and reduceing its overall performance at a time when it was up against better American aircraft in the Grumman F6F Hellcat, the

upper left: Japanese Vice-Admiral Takejiro Onishi strongly advocated the kamikaze idea; upper right: Kamikaze pilots in 1945; left: A Japanese bomb explodes on the flight deck of the USS *Enterprise*, killing the photographer Robert F. Read.

Vought F4U Corsair, and the Lockheed P-38J Lightning. The ultimate Zero, the A6M8c, came into production in 1945 near the end of the war. It was considered a higher altitude solution with a 355 mph top speed, and an improved rate of climb, but it arrived too late to be of much use. The improvements featured in that final version might have might have made somewhat of a difference to Japanese military aviation in the war had they appeared much sooner, but the enormous losses in equipment and pilots that Japan incurred in the latter half of the war, coupled with her very limited production capability by that point, meant she was being massively out-produced in the field of fighter aircraft by the Allies. In all its variants, 10,936 Zero fighters were built, compared to 13, 700 Curtiss P-40s, 12,200 Grumman Hellcats, 12,500 Vought Corsairs, 15,300 Republic P-47 Thunderbolts, 14,000 Hawker Hurricanes and Sea Hurricanes, 10,000 Lockheed P-38 Lightnings, 15,000 North American P-51 Mustangs, and 22,800 Spitfires and Seafires.

Many years after the Second World War, the former fighter pilot ace Saburo Sakai visited the Champlin Fighter Museum in Mesa, Arizona, where he was treated to a ride in P-51 Mustang. During the flight he had the opportunity to take the controls for a while. Until that moment he had always believed in the Mitsubishi Zero which was, to him, the best fighter plane anywhere, ever. The experience of flying the Mustang changed his mind. He came away feeling that the wonderful, high-performance P-51 was number one with him. The Zero was relegated to number two.

He was descended from the Samurai, the ancient warrior class of Japan, who lived by the code of Bushido, serving the lords of the prefecture and living so as to always be prepared to die. Saburo Sakai was the third of four sons. His father died when he was eleven and he was adopted by an uncle who agreed to provide the boy with a good education. But Saburo's prior educational accomplishment was soon forgotten when he was unable to achieve high scholarship in his new academic environment. This, together with his choice of unsavory friends in the new school, brought shame on his family and his uncle, who sent him home in disgrace. He felt that his entire village had been disgraced by his behaviour and lack of achievement at school, and he decided he could not remain there. So in 1933, at the age of sixteen, he joined the Japanese Navy and soon reported to the Sasebo Naval Base for initial training.

Saburo described his naval training experience as a brutal one. The young recruits were beaten with sticks for the slightest infraction: "I remember sometimes passing out from the blows. The body and mind can take only so much punishment. We were [expected] to suffer in silence. Although there were some [Petty Officers] who were sadistic, there was a method in all of this madness. It made us tough as nails, and in battle this is often the decisive factor. After the first six months we were completely automated in our manner. We dared not, or even thought about questioning orders or authority, no matter how rediculous the order.

On graduating from his basic training, Sakai was assigned to the battleship *Kirishima* as a turret gunner. In 1935 he studied for and passed the naval gunnery school exam and was soon assigned to the battleship *Haruna*, a Petty Officer 3rd Class.

Recalling his entry to naval flight training: "There were three ways to enter flight school in the early days. Remember that the recruiting method in the time before 1941 was very different than after we were at war with the United States. The need for pilots caused the quality to drop steeply as the war went on. However, in 1937 when I was selected, there were three ways to get in: Officers graduating from the Naval Academy at Eta Jima; Petty Officers from the fleet; and young men recruited from the

left: A dramatic photograph capturing the instant of a kamikaze plane striking the flight deck of a U.S. Navy carrier; below: U.S. Navy crews firing 40mm anti-aircraft guns at attacking kamikazes.

left: Trailing a fiery plume, the end of a kamikaze attack on an American warship; right: The aircraft of a Japanese attacker scores a direct hit on this Essex class U.S. carrier; below: Members of the Japanese Army Air Force Tokko Tai had to take a major part in the kamikaze attacks when most of the Japanese Navy pilots had been killed in the suicide raids.

832 crew members of the carrier USS *Franklin* died when the ship was hit by two Japanese bombs during a kamikaze attack on 19 March 1945. The *Franklin* and her crew were the most decorated in U.S. Navy history. They sailed the devastated carrier 12,000 miles to the Brooklyn Navy Yard for her major repairs; Japanese naval aviators, upper right: Kaneyoshi Muto; lower right: Hiroyoshi Nishizawa.

A kamikaze narrowly misses the crowded flight deck of the U.S. Navy escort carrier *Sangamon* in May 1945.

schools who would start their careers as pilots (similar to the American ROTC program today).

"Pilot selection was very strict; the men chosen in 1937 when I was selected were a different breed. The men selected to fly in 1944-45 would not have been qualified to even pump fuel into my aircraft at this time, if that shows how select the program was. I remember that 1,500 men had applied for training, and seventy had been selected that year. I was one of them, and all were non-commissioned officers from the fleet. This does not include the ensigns coming from the academy; they had their own selection process. That year I do not believe any civilian recruits were chosen, but that would change as the war with America continued. I was twenty years old; I knew that my acceptance into flight school dismissed my previous dishonor, and my uncle and family were proud of me. The entire village was proud of me." Saburo began his flight training in 1936. Of the twenty-five students in his class, he ranked first. Upon graduating: "We had additional training in land and aircraft carrier landings at the Naval bases of Oita and Omura in Kyushu, and instrument flying was stressed heavily. This cannot be underestimated, for it saved my life in 1942. This training lasted three months, although I never flew from a carrier during the war. I was sent to southeastern China and in May 1938 I had my first combat.

Just hours after the Japanese attack on U.S. ships and facilities at Pearl Harbor, Hawaii ... on 8 December 1941, Sakai was one of forty-five Zero pilots to attack Clark airfield in the Philippines. He was awakened at 0200, but their take-off was delayed by a heavy fog. The pilots had breakfast and waited at their aircraft. There they were told of the attacks on Pearl Harbor and the Aleutians, and Sakai wondered if the Americans at Clark Field would be expecting their attack. Finally, at mid-morning, Sakai and the other pilots of Tainan Squadron were ordered to take off. They got off to a bad start when one of the bombers they were to escort in the raid crashed on take-off, killing its entire crew.

When Sakai and his fellow pilots reached 19,000 feet, he spotted a formation of U.S. Army Air Corps bombers heading towards his squadron's airfield. The Japanese pilots flying top cover had orders to attack any aircraft approaching their base, which they headed off to do while the other Japanese aircraft continued on towards the Clark Field target. He and the others in his flight soon realized that the bombers they were about to attack were, in fact, Japanese Army aircraft on a routine flight. The pilots of Tainan Squadron had not been informed about them and had come close to being involved in a major accident of war.

The pilots reformed and, arriving over Clark Field, were surprised that they had not been intercepted. They observed five U.S. fighters below them, but they were under orders not to engage the enemy until all the Japanese bombers were in the area. Sakai was amazed that the American aircraft on the field were parked in perfect alignment, making the Japanese bombing and strafing attack relatively easy and heavily destructive. He then sighted two B-17 Flying Fortress bombers and made a strafing run on them. It was then that he and two other pilots were jumped by the five American P-40 fighters they had seen earlier. In this, his first air combat experience against the Americans, Saburo managed to shoot down one of the fighters. The squadron had destroyed thirty-five American aircraft on the ground.

On 10 December, Sakai's was one of twenty-seven Zero fighters flying a sweep towards Clark Field. At the same time, a B-17 bomber piloted by Captain Colin Kelly, Jr, had been hit by gunfire from the Japanese cruiser Natori as the plane was returning to the Clark base from a bombing mission. The B-17 was seriously damaged and when the Zeros of the Tainan group encountered it, Sakai and the others attacked it. Kelly, and his co-pilot, Lt Donald Robins, remained at the controls of the B-17 so the other crew members could bail out. As Kelly and Robins attempted to escape the bomber, it exploded. Robins survived, his parachute opening just in time. Kelly's did not. Theirs was the first American B-17 bomber of the war to be shot down.

There are stories about Sakai; they may or may not be true. But one that persists and certainly has the ring of truth about it is the story of a former Dutch military nurse who happened to be flying low in a Dutch military C-47, Dakota to English readers, over the jungle of Java in 1942. The plane was an air ambulance; the cargo several wounded soldiers and children, being evacuated from a combat area to receive better treatment elsewhere. Seemingly from out of nowhere, a Japanese Zero fighter appeared near the C-47. So close was the enemy fighter that the nurse could clearly see his facial features as he brought the fighter quite near alongside the much larger plane. The nurse, together with some of the children, were riveted by the sight of the enemy, almost within touching distance, and apparently threatening to kill them with a few well-placed rounds from his guns. They began waving frantically to him in the slight hope that he would spare their lives. This strange communication went on for what must have seemed an eternity to the nurse and the children, but was actually but a moment or two. At last, the Japanese pilot wobbled his wings to let them know they would live, before he peeled off and disappeared from view. The nurse and the children cheered and cried in relief that their terror had ended happily.

After more than fifty years and considerable effort on her part, the Dutch nurse finally tracked down the pilot of that Zero fighter, Saburo Sakai. With great luck and determination, and the help of the Japanese Red Cross who managed to locate Sakai. He had been on a routine combat air patrol the day of the encounter with the C-47. The Red Cross person interviewing him asked if he recalled the incident. He said that he did and that he had briefly considered shooting down the C-47, because the Japanese High Command had ordered fighter patrols to down any and all enemy aircraft they encountered, whether they were armed or not. But when he saw the waving hands and the panic-stricken expressions on the clearly innocent faces in the windows of the big transport plane, he relented and spared their lives.

As a fighter pilot, Sakai's job was to seek out and destroy the enemies of his nation. But he was a human being as well, fully capable of mercy and compassion, while also equipped with the killer instinct. When faced with a decision about the C-47 enemy aircraft, he thought about his orders, about the military value of such a "kill", and about what he believed was the right thing to do, and he departed.

Saburo Sakai died on 22 September, 2000. In his obituary of the Japanese World War Two fighter ace, Douglas Martin wrote in The New York Times: "Of the 150 pilots who began in his unit, only three survived the war. In August 1942, he was hit in the face by a bullet from a Grumman Avenger torpedo bomber. He was blinded in the right eye and his left side was paralyzed. He was prepared to die. Mr Sakai was one of the few Japanese servicemen to rise from the ranks of enlisted men to officer."

After the war, as an act of atonement, Mr Sakai became a lay Buddhist acolyte and claimed that since then he had not killed any creature, not even a mosquito.

"It is absolutely out of the question for you to return alive. Your mission involves certain death. Your bodies will be dead, but not your spirits. The death of a single one of you will be the birth of a million others. Neglect nothing that may affect your training or your health. You must not leave behind

Struck twice within thirty minutes by kamikazes, the carrier USS *Bunker Hill* is an inferno.

any cause for regret, which would follow you into eternity. And, lastly: do not be in too much of a hurry to die. If you cannot find your target, turn back; next time you may find a more favorable opportunity. Choose a death which brings about a maximum result."
—from The First Order to the Kamikaze

"I would attack any squadron blockading a port. Nothing could prevent me from dropping out of the clear blue sky onto a battleship, with 400 kilos of explosives in the cockpit. Of course, it is true that the pilot would be killed, but everything would blow up, and that's what counts."
—Jules Vedrines, pre-1914 French aviation pioneer

In the final months of 1944, Imperial Japan was losing the war, and some of its military leaders began to express the belief that desperate times called for desperate measures. The notion of self-sacrifice for Emperor and country was commonly accepted among the Japanese, and suicide per se was not alien, and was honoured for its purity by many who had been raised on tales of heroic Samurai warriors. So, it was but a short step to the concept of suicide as a weapon. One example of that concept was the Kaiten human torpedo. Fifty-four feet long and carrying a 3,000-pound warhead, the Kaiten had a range of thirty miles at slow speed, or twelve miles at its top speed of forty knots. The launch of a Kaiten was a one-way trip for the crew, who could not get out. Most of the Kaitens proved unstable and only one Allied vessel was sunk by the weapon, the tanker USS *Mississinewa*.

At this time, a General Yashida of the Japanese Army Air Force, was promoting the use of suicidal air attacks and training in ramming techniques was secretly included in the pilot training syllabus. One Japanese Army General Yoshiroko, commanding units in the Solomon Islands, was frustrated by the ineffectiveness of the anti-tank weapons in his arsenal. He ordered his troops to strap satchels of explosives to their bodies and dive under the tanks of the American enemy. Results were not what the general had expected, and he was severely criticised by the High Command in Tokyo. But the Japanese concept and use of "human bullets" continued.

"The code of the Samurai demands that we must always be ready to die, but that does not mean we must commit suicide on the slightest pretext. Our tradition desires that we should live and fight as best we can so as to experience neither regret nor remorse at the moment of death."
—a Kamikaze instructor quoted in *L'Epopée Kamikaze* by Bernard Millot

Vice-Admiral Takejiro Onishi, Imperial Japanese Navy, was a principal advocate of the kamikaze idea.

It was he who originated the name kamikaze, which means Divine Wind and is believed to be a reference to the ancient winds that sank the threatening Mongol fleet. Kamikaze pilots were members of special attack units. Their mission was to become human bombs—one with their aeroplanes—and sacrifice themselves by diving their planes into enemy ships with the goal of sinking them.

In an effort to instill high morale among his airmen, the vice-admiral introduced some ceremonial aspects to the kamikaze units, including the pre-flight toast of sacred water—later changed to saki—and the wearing of a decorated white headband called a *hachimaki,* a touch of Samurai, indicating that the warrior was prepared to fight to the death. The majority also wore a *sennin-bari*, a silk or cloth band stitched with red threads that was said to have the power of a bullet-proof vest. Most kamikaze pilots carried a personal flag, usually a small square of white cloth with a red *hinomaru* circle in the centre and calligraphy encouraging "a suicide spirit". Kamikaze pilots and their families received privileges, including extra food rations, as well as "very honourable" status. Some referred to the kamikaze as "the black-edged cherry blossoms".

Onishi was concerned about the shortage of skilled Japanese pilots, but still believed in the suicide weapon idea. "If a pilot facing a ship or plane exhausts all his resources, he still has his plane left as a part of himself. What greater glory than to give his life for emperor and country?"

In *Kamikaze—Japan's Suicide Samurai,* author Raymond Lamont-Brown states:
"... the kamikaze pilots evolved from four main sources of recruitment. First came the 'patriotic crusaders' who were all volunteers, usually from daimyo or samurai families; they were motivated by nationalistic fervour, military ideals and the concept of chivalry upon which their ancestors had based personal sacrifice to fulfil perceived duties to the state. From this group evolved the ritualization of the kamikaze before suicide flights (i.e., the wearing of samurai symbols, singing patriotic songs, writing poetry glorifying kamikaze action, composing testamentory last letters home, distributing personal effects, and so on.

"Next came the 'nation's face savers'. These were recruits who did volunteer, but often for negative reasons, to avoid personal shame in not emulating the deaths of the patriotic crusaders, or to espouse military heroism in order to save the *kami* land of Japan from humiliating defeat. Like the

far left: A direct hit on a U.S. Navy aircraft carrier; centre: An A6M Zero ploughs into the flank of the battleship USS *Missouri* on 11 April 1945; left: In a kamikaze attack on 25 October 1944, the U.S. escort carrier *St Lo* sank after torpedos stored in the hangar deck exploded, blowing the stern off the ship.

patriotic crusaders, they too were conformists to the traditions of Japanese society. As the kamikaze Susumu Kitjitsu (1923-45) was to write to his parents: 'I live quite a normal life. Death does not frighten me; my only care is to know if I am going to be able to sink an aircraft carrier by crashing into it.'

"By the last few months of the war the third category of recruits emerged: these were the 'young rationalists'. They came mostly straight from higher education, went through hurried training and died to sustain the war effort and to keep Japan free from foreign taint. As Bernard Millot wrote: 'With a few very rare exceptions, they were the most affectionate, well-educated, least troublesome sons who gave their parents the greatest satisfaction.'

"The last group of recruits were also mostly young, the 'appointed daredevils', who emerged right at the end of the war. It may be noted that among their number were do-or-die delinquents, hell-raisers and those of shady moral reputation and social deviation who, through the drastic measure of suicide, were escaping the legal, civic, and social consequences of their behaviour."

"The psychology behind [the kamikaze attacks] was too alien to us. Americans who fight to live, find it hard to realize that another people will fight to die."
—Admiral William F. Halsey, Commander, U.S. Third Fleet

Onishi could not actually order his pilots to fly the special suicide attacks. They had to volunteer, and with no expectation of survival, they did so almost unanimously. On 20 October 1944, he addressed twenty-six fighter pilot volunteers who were to comprise the Shimpu (God and Wind) Force: "My sons, who can raise our country from the desperate situation in which she finds herself? Japan is in grave danger. The salvation of our country is now beyond the power of the Ministers of State, the General Staff, and lowly commanders like myself. It can come only from spirited young men such as you. Thus on behalf of your hundred million countrymen, I ask you this sacrifice, and pray for your success. You are already gods, without earthly desires. But one thing you want to know is that your own crash-dive is not in vain. Regrettably, we will not be able to tell you the results. But I shall watch your efforts to the end and report your deeds to the Throne. You may all rest assured on this point. I ask you to do your best."

Shortly after Onishi's speech, 201st Air Group Chusa Tadashi Nakajima was assigned to Cebu in the Philippines. His job there was to set up a new kamikaze unit. When he arrived he told his pilots there: "I have come here to organize another Special Attack Unit. Others will want to follow in the footsteps of the first pilots charged with this mission. Any non-commissioned officer or enlisted flyer who wishes to volunteer will so signify by writing his name and rate on a piece of paper. Each piece of paper is to be placed in an envelope which will be delivered to me by 2100 hours today. It is not expected, however, that everyone should volunteer. We know that you are all willing to die in defence of your country. We also realize that some of you, because of your family situation, cannot be expected to offer your life in this way. You should understand also that the number of volunteers required is limited by the small number of planes available. Whether a man volunteers or not will be known only to me. I ask that each man, within the next three hours, come to a decision based entirely upon his own situation. Special Attack operations will be ready to start tomorrow. Because secrecy in this operation is of utmost importance, there must be no discussion about it." All of the pilots volunteered.

Vice-Admiral Onishi launched a mass of kamikaze attacks in November 1944. On the 5th one of his groups of aircraft was on its way to strike at an American landing force on Leyte. It encountered

By March 1945, the Japanese were down to a small number of airmen, "pilots" who were barely able to fly at all, having had minimal training. The remaining force of kamikaze and conventional bombers in the area was ordered on 17 March to strike with the greatest possible intensity at the American fleet, which was less than 100 miles from the coast of Japan. In that attack on the U.S. carrier *Franklin*, the crew suffered more than 1,000 casualties. The Japanese lost fifty-two more aircraft.

a large formation of U.S. bombers and all of the Japanese pilots rammed their aircraft into their American enemies. Then, in a desperate effort to prevent the American invasion of Luzon, Onishi diverted his pilots from their planned attacks on U.S. aircraft carriers, to striking transport vessels, and he started the practice of using heavy bombers loaded with explosives in his suicide units. Later in the month, his kamikazes flew against the American carriers, causing serious damage to four, forcing the U.S. Command to increase the number of its destroyers on picket duty around the carriers, as well as doubling the number of fighters flying combat air patrols from them. American sailors going on shore leave had orders not to discuss the kamikaze attacks. The American bombing of Japanese airfields on Luzon was increased. The U.S. forces were dealt another blow in mid-December when a major typhoon hit the Philippines heavily damaging many American warships, leaving much of the fleet in port for repairs. Onishi was not fairing much better, having fewer planes than pilots by this time. He determined to order all pilots without planes to fight on as infantry when the forces of the enemy landed on Luzon. That invasion began on 9 January. By the 13th, 1,208 Japanese pilots had died in kamikaze missions. The only option available to the U.S. Navy warship crews lay in putting up a maximum concentration of gunfire at the incoming suicide planes.

In January, Admiral Onishi was reassigned to Formosa to rapidly organize more new kamikaze units. The Japanese now focused on destroying the American fleet in order to force some kind of hon-ourable peace settlement, and the kamikaze pilots were at the centre of that action. American B-29 bombers, "Mr B" to the Japanese, were ramping up their massive bombing campaign against Japan's home islands and on 9 March they struck an immense blow at Tokyo, killing nearly 100,000 Japanese and making more than one million homeless. In an attempted retaliatory strike on U.S. Navy ships in the huge American harbour at Ulithi by kamikaze and Japanese bombers, they achieved little success. Now utterly desperate, the Japanese military planners saw only two choices: surrender, or fight to the death making maximum use of the kamikaze weapon. The latter option gained more and more favour as the B-29 fire raids were staged with ever greater intensity. Time was running out for the Japanese though, as was their supply of aircraft, fuel and, of course, pilots. By March they were down to a small number of airmen, "pilots" who were barely able to fly at all, having had minimal training. The remain-ing force of kamikaze and conventional Japanese bombers in the area was ordered on 17 March to strike with the greatest possible intensity at the U.S. fleet, which was then less than 100 miles south of the Japanese mainland. In that attack, the U.S. Navy carrier *Franklin* was very badly hit and the crew suffered more than 1,000 casualties. The Japanese lost fifty-two more aircraft.

"If destruction be our lot we must ourselves be its author and finisher. As a nation of free men we must live through all time, or die by suicide."
—from a speech by Abraham Lincoln, 27 January 1838, at Springfield, Illinois

Dear Parents,
Please congratulate me. I have been given a splendid opportunity to die. This is my last day. The des-tiny of our homeland hinges on the decisive battle in the sea to the south where I shall fall like a blos-som from a radiant cherry tree.
—from a last letter home in *The Divine Wind* by Captain Rikihei Inoguichi and Commander Tadashi Nakajima, with Roger Pineau

In 1956 Jean Larteguy's edited version of the George Blond description of a typical kamikaze attack in *Le Survivant du Pacifique* appeared in Larteguy's *The Sun Goes Down*: "On 14 May, at 6.50 a.m., the radar plotter reported an isolated 'blip', bearing 200° at 8,000 feet, range about twenty miles. The rear guns were pointed in that direction, ready to fire as soon as the 'phantom' should appear. At 6.54 it came into sight, flying straight for the carrier. It disappeared for a moment in the clouds; then, after approximately three and a half miles, it emerged again, losing altitude. It was a Zero. The five-inch guns opened fire. The Japanese aircraft retreated into the clouds. The batteries continued to fire. The crew had been at action stations since four in the morning. All the aircraft that were not in the air had been de-fuelled and parked below decks.

"The Japanese machine approached from the rear. It was still not to be seen, as it was hidden by the clouds. Guided by radar, the five-inch guns continued to fire at it, and soon the 40mm machine-guns began to fire as well. It was very strange to see all these guns firing relentlessly at an invisible enemy.

"The Japanese aircraft emerged from the clouds and began to dive. His angle of incidence was not more than 30°, his speed approximately 250 knots. There could be no doubt—it was a suicide plane. It was approaching quite slowly and deliberately, and manoeuvring just enough not to be hit too soon.

"The pilot knew his job thoroughly and all those who watched him make his approach felt their mouths go dry. In less than a minute he would have attained his goal, there could be little doubt that this man was to crash his machine on the deck [of the carrier *Enterprise*, CV-6].

"All the batteries were firing; the five-inch guns, the 40mm and the 20mm, even the rifles. The Japanese aircraft dived through a rain of steel. It had been hit in several places and seemed to be trailing a banner of flame and smoke, but it came on, clearly visible, hardly moving, the line of its wings as straight as a sword.

"The deck was deserted; every man, with the exception of the gunners, was lying flat on his face. Flaming and roaring, the fireball passed in front of the 'island' and crashed with a terrible impact just behind the for'ard lift.

"The entire vessel was shaken, some forty yards of the flight deck folded up like a banana-skin: an enormous piece of the lift, at least a third of the platform, was thrown over 300 feet into the air. The explosion killed fourteen men. The last earthly impression they took with them was the picture of the kamikaze trailing his banner of flame and increasing in size with lightning rapidity.

"The mortal remains of the pilot had not disappeared. They had been laid out in a corner of the deck, next to the blackened debris of the machine. The entire crew marched past the corpse of the volunteer of death. The men were less interested in his finely modelled features, his wide-open eyes which were now glazed over, than in the buttons on his tunic, which were to become wonderful souvenirs of the war for a few privileged officers of high rank. These buttons, now black, were stamped in relief with the insignia of the kamekaze corps: a cherry blossom with three petals."

On Kudan Hill in the heart of Tokyo, near the Imperial Palace, stands the Yasukuni-jinja, or Shrine for Establishing Peace in the Empire. It is dedicated to Japan's war dead and is a controversial war memorial because it contains personal effects of executed war criminals, including Hideki Tojo. "Even today," according to Raymond Lamont-Brown, "any government minister who makes an official visit to the shrine would be technically liable to be stripped of his office." Displays in the Yasukuni include relics of the kamikaze pilots of the Great East Asian War, as the Japanese refer to the Second World War. Japanese war veterans groups, as well as representatives of the Bereaved Families Association, regularly visit the shrine and petition the public to sign requests for the Yasukuni to be reinstated as the official Japanese war memorial. Lamont-Brown states: 'As time passes, according to some sections of the Japanese press, the spirits of the dead kamikaze 'cry out' for honourable, official recognition through the members of the 'Thunder Gods Association' who meet annually at the Yasukuni-jinja on 21 March—the day on which the first Ohka suicide attack was made.' "

In the last days before their final attacks, the kamikaze pilots were mostly calmed by the Bushido philosophy. They were able to relax in a seeming detachment, spending their waiting time listening to gramophone records, playing cards, reading, and writing their last letters home. They gave their belongings to comrades and friends, and they all carried three sen in copper coins, their fare to cross the Japanese equivalent of the River Styx.

"I was wired to the port catapult of the *San Jacinto*, when the boing boing boing went off, followed by 'This is no drill!' I saw a Japanese Jill aircraft coming across the front of our ship, starboard to port. He was low, about 100 feet, and every ship in the fleet was shooting at him. I started yelling at the catapult officer to launch my plane. It seemed to take forever. I charged my guns while waiting. The Japanese plane had bore-sighted another carrier to our port side. Finally the cat fired. The Jill, with bomb or torpedo in plain view, was crossing my launch path. I squeezed the trigger. Nothing. The gear was still down. The guns are not supposed to fire with the gear down. I hit the gear-up lever. The Jill was closing at full deflection. I was squeezing the trigger. At last all six .50s were firing just as the Jill crossed in front of me. It exploded as it flew into my line of fire. I had been in the air less than thirty seconds. My aircraft was hit several times by shrapnel, but I continued my combat air patrol and landed just under four hours later."
—former U.S. Navy fighter pilot James B. Cain, 19 March 1945

Japanese naval aviators, far upper left: Toshio Ota; far upper right: Sadaaki Akamatsu; lower left: Toshiaki Honda; lower right: Masuaki Endo; left: Damaged Japanese military aircraft in a Pacific field at war's end.

An EA-1F Spad Skyraider pilot throttles up to full power as the cat officer signals for launch on the USS *Intrepid.*

The three-year United Nations "police action' from June 1950 through June 1953 on the Korean peninsula involved many attack missions flown by American and British naval aviators, most of whom had incurred air combat experience in World War Two. In the Korean conflict, these men struck at and savaged the infrastructure of their North Korean enemy, destroying eighty-three enemy aircraft, 313 bridges, 262 junks and river craft, 220 locomotives, 1,421 rail cars, 163 tanks, nearly 3,000 support vehicles, and 12,789 military buildings. They utilized their considerable WW2 experience to accomplish these feats in Korea, a U.N. action which was only approved by that body in the absence of member nation the Soviet Union which happened to be boycotting the U.N. Security Council when the Council approved going to war against the invading forces of North Korea. Had they been present for that vote, the Soviets would have undoubtedly used their veto to prevent the United Nations from acting.

John Bolt had flown U.S. Marine Corps Vought F4U Corsair fighters in the Pacific campaign during WW2 and had been officially credited with downing six Japanese Zeke fighters. He would become the only Navy Department jet ace of the Korean War, in which he shot down six MiG-15 fighters.

Bolt, known as Jack, still felt the need for speed and air action in 1950 when the North Koreans moved south to kindle war in Korea: "I chose an Air Force exchange tour of duty because at that point the only thing standing up to the MiG-15s were the F-86s. I knew that none were coming to the Marine Corps, and I was anxious to get back to the air-to-air fight. The only possibility of doing that was by getting in an F-86 squadron. The MiGs were beating the hell out of everything else, and the F-86s were our sole air superiority plane in Korea from early on. So I managed to get a year's tour with the Air Force, and toward the end of it I managed to get into an F-86 squadron of the Oregon Air National Guard.

"I would grind out the hours in that thing, standing air defense alerts. Those were the days when the threat of nuclear war with Russia hung heavily over our heads. We really thought we were going to get into it. It was late 1951 or early 1952 and the squadron was part of the Northwest Air Defense Command. Our guys were on standby and would be down in the ready room in flight gear, not sitting in the planes the way they did later. They would be playing bridge and so forth, but I would be up flying, getting hours in that F-86. When my guard tour was over, I was able to get out to Korea in about May of '52 and flew ninety-four missions in F9F-4 Panthers, interdictions, air-to-ground, and close air support. We were down at K-3, an airfield near Po Hang Do, with VMF-115.

"We were using napalm to attack rice-straw thatched-roof targets. They were all supposed to contain enemy troops, but I'm sure most of them were probably innocent civilians. We were attacking the villages with napalm. Then, of course, the proper military targets used thatching for waterproofing too, a supply depot for food or materiel, fuel or ammo. We used lots of napalm against all of those targets.

"My tour in Panthers came to an end and I took some R and R. I looked up an Air Force squadron commander named George Ruddell. I had met him at El Toro in 1947 when he flew an F-80 over to lecture our squadron about it and give us a little demonstration of what that airplane could do. I found George at K-13 where he was commanding the 39th Fighter Interceptor Squadron. I told him about my 100 hours in the F-86F, the same type of Sabre his squadron was flying. I had the experience he needed, and he was friendly towards me and let me take a few fam flights with some of his boys. On a second R and R trip around Christmas of '52, it happened that Joe McConnell, who was to become the top-scoring U.S. fighter ace of the Korean War with sixteen kills, had just been grounded from operations, and Ruddell very generously sent him over to teach me some tactics. I flew a few fam hops with McConnell and he was good. We became friends and he taught me a lot about his tactics in the F-86. He was very deserving of the fame that he had earned as the leading ace of that war. Tragically, he was killed soon after the war on a test flight at Edwards Air Force Base in California.

"After that second R and R, I put in for another Air Force exchange tour. The Group Personnel Officer said: 'Bolt, I know you've been trying to worm your way into this, going up there on R and R. I'll tell you, you've had a year with the Air Force and you ain't goin' up there. You think you are. I'm telling you now, it ain't gonna happen.' They felt that I'd had more than my share of gravy assignments, so I got in touch with Ruddell and he got the general up there to send a wire down to the Marine Corps general. They only had two F-86 groups, the 4th and the 51st, and they had two Marines in each. One of them, a guy named Roy Reed, was leaving shortly. This was the opening I needed. The Air Force general's wire read: 'We're willing to have your pilots, but they come up here having never flown the plane, and they present a training burden on our people. But now we have a rare instance of having a pilot who's shown enough initiative to come up here and get checked out, and he's ready to go. Would you mind appointing John Bolt?'

"There was nothing else the group could do. I was put in Ruddell's squadron and I was flying on McConnell's wing for my first half dozen flights. I was in Dog Flight. Ruddell was a very tough guy, but he was as nice as he could be. He had four or five kills, but the MiGs had stopped coming south of the Yalu River and we weren't allowed to go north of it. The Chinese were yelling about the 'pirates' that were coming over there, but that's where the action was.

"When McConnell left, I took over the command of Dog Flight, a quarter of the squadron with about twelve pilots. We lived in one big Quonset hut.

"Ruddell wasn't getting any MiGs because they weren't coming south of the river. He'd been threatening everybody that he'd kill 'em, cut their heads off if they went north of the river after MiGs. But one night he weakened. He'd had a few drinks and he called me into this little cubbyhole where he had his quarters. During the discussion tears came to his eyes—running down his cheeks—as he was saying how he wanted to be a good Air Force officer, and he loved the Air Force, and if they told him to do something, he'd do it, and if they told him not to do something, he'd not do it. But getting those MiGs meant more to him than his career and life itself. And, since he had been beating up on his own flight about not going across the river, he'd be embarrassed to ask any of them to go across it with him. He didn't know whether they would want to anyway—two or three members of Dog Flight didn't like to do it. They would have been in big trouble if they'd been identified as going up there. I don't know if the ones they picked up later on, who were shot down north of the river, were ever disciplined when the war was over. But at the time, the threat was believed and hanging very heavily over us. Ruddell said: 'Would you give me some of your flight? I want to go across the river. I've gotta have some action.' Ruddell's boys had been several days with no action. I said, 'Sure, I'd be delighted', so we planned one for the next day.

"I was to fly his second section. On a river crossing flight, we would take off and go full bore. We'd fly those planes at 100 per cent power setting until we got out of combat. Engine life was planned for 800 hours and we were getting about 550 or so. Turbine blade cracks were developing. We were running the engines at maximum temperature. You could put these little constrictors in the tailpipe—we called them 'rats'—and you could 'rat 'em up' until they ran at maximum temperature. They were real

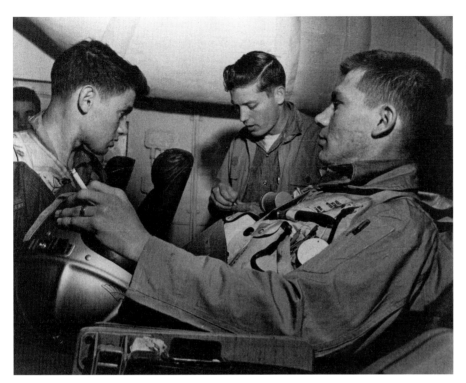

hot rods. You'd run your drop tanks dry just about the time you got up to the river, and if you didn't have a contact, you weren't supposed to drop your tanks. We skinned 'em every time anyway.

"On at least four occasions, by the end of the flight I had been to over 50,000 feet. When it was empty and I still hadn't pulled the power back from 100 per cent, the airplane would really get up there. The MiG-15 could get right up there too.

"On the flight with Ruddell, we got up there and dropped our tanks. At least the pilots going across the river dropped them. There were big clouds up as we crossed the river. It was early morning and we heard on the radio that there was a fight going on. There were some MiGs flying this day. We came from the sunny side of the clouds to the backside of a big cumulous; there were some black puffs of flak and there were some planes down there. We were half blind from the diminished illumination on the backside of the cloud. It was a confusing situation. We drove down and there was a MiG. Ruddell got it in sight and we dropped from 43,000 feet down to about 15,000, just dropped straight down. He got into shooting position behind the MiG, but didn't shoot … didn't shoot … didn't shoot. I tore past him and blew up the MiG. I had experience at jumping planes and one of the things you did when you came down from extreme altitude (MiGs were frequently found down low when north of the river) was put your armour-glass defrost on full bore. It would get so hot it was almost painful, but it kept the front windscreen clear. You also tested your guns and your G-suit. Ruddell's windscreen had fogged over. He was sitting there in a kill position and couldn't see properly to shoot. So, I went by him and got the MiG. Of course, the squadron was abuzz that the Colonel had started crossing the river and gotten aced out of his first kill up there. I was a MiG-killer. I'd gotten three or four. When I got back, they had all these signs pasted up all over the Dog Flight Quonset hut. One read: 'Marine wetback steals Colonel's MiG.'

"The 'kill rules' were, if you got seven hits on an enemy aircraft, you would be given a kill. The MiGs didn't torch off at high altitude; they simply would not burn because of the air density. So, incendiary hits would be counted (we had good gun cameras) and if you got seven hits in the enemy's fuselage, the odds were it was dead, and they'd give you a kill. We knew that every third round was an incendiary so, in effect, if you got three incendiary hits showing on the gun camera film, it was considered a dead MiG.

"My first kill was at about 43,000 feet. I had missed a couple of kills before it by not being aggressive or determined enough. I was almost desperate for a MiG kill. I was leader of my flight and I'd screwed up a couple of bounces. My self-esteem and my esteem in the Flight were low, and I decided that the next MiG I saw was a dead man and I didn't care where he was.

"The next MiG was part of a gaggle; MiGs as far as you could see. I made a good run on one of them and pulled into firing position, but other MiGs were shooting at me and my wingman, and they were very close. I got some hits on my MiG and he went into a scissor, which was a good tactic. I think

Just time to write a letter home.

the F-86 may have had a better roll rate. I was trying to shoot as he passed through my firing angle. Each time I fired I delayed my turn, so he was gaining on me and drifting back. He almost got behind me and was so close that his plane blanked out the camera frame. I think he realized that I would have crashed into him rather than let him get behind me, and he rolled out and dove. Then I got several more hits on him and he pulled up (he was probably dead at this point). That scissor was the right thing to do; he just shouldn't have broken off. He was getting back to a position where he could have taken the advantage.

"The salvation of the F-86 was that it had good transsonic controls; the MiG's controls were sub-sonic. In the Sabre, you could readily cruise at about .84 Mach. The MiG had to go into its uncontrol-lable range to attack you, and its stick forces were unmanageable. As I recall, the kill ratio between the F-86 and the MiG was eight to one. This was due almost entirely to the flying tail of the Sabre, although it had other superior features. The gun package of the MiG was intended for shooting down bombers like the B-29 and B-50. It carried a 37mm and two 23mm cannons, which was overkill against fight-ers. Although the F-86 used essentially the same machine-guns as a World War Two fighter, the rate of fire had been doubled, and it was a very good package against other fighters.

"Down low, where we were out of the transsonic superiority range, we wore a G-suit and they didn't. You can fight defensively when you are blacked out, but you can't fight offensively. If you had enough speed to pull a good 6G turn, you would 'go black' in twenty to thirty degrees of the turn. The MiG pilot couldn't follow you because he was blacked out too. You are still conscious, though you have three to five seconds of vision loss. When you had gone about as far in the turn as you thought you could carry it, you could pop the stick forward and your vision would immediately return. You had already started your roll, and the MiG was right there in front of you, every time, because, not having a G-suit, he had eased off in the turn. His G-tolerance was only half of yours. So he was right there and most probably would overshoot you."

Paul Ludwig, a former U.S. Navy attack pilot: "With little more than a hundred hours in the AD Skyraider, I got orders to an AD squadron on the west coast. After I got there I wanted some addi-tional cross-country time so a friend and I flew our Skyraiders up the coast to NAS Alameda near Oakland. While over Los Angeles that night I felt very uneasy because everywhere I looked all I could see was a sea of lights. Over Los Angeles is not the place to lose an engine in a single-engine airplane. There was no place to set down if the engine quit. For several long minutes we flew along over that huge city with me thinking that if the engine quit I would have to ride that free-falling anvil into any unlighted patch I could find. I didn't want to drop an AD into a house. There were no black holes to be seen."

Bill Hannan was a U.S. Navy jet engine mechanic in the 1950s: "During the Korean War, our task force was operating in concert with other carriers, the *Boxer, Bon Homme Richard, Philippine Sea, Oriskany, Princeton, Valley Forge* and *Essex*. It wasn't unusual for a fatigued pilot, returning from a stressful mis-sion, to land on the wrong ship, in spite of the huge identification number painted on their flight decks. When it happened on our carrier, the *Kearsarge*, the errant aviator had to suffer the humiliation of returning to his own ship with derisive graffiti painted all over his airplane, such as: NO, WE DON'T SERVE BEER HERE EITHER, and ROSES ARE RED, VIOLETS ARE BLUE, THIS IS THE KEARSARGE, WHO ARE YOU?"

Frank Furbish, former U.S. Navy pilot: "Cat shots never bothered me. You are as much passenger as pilot. Even if you shut down the engines and set the parking brake, you were going off the cat. Just five knots slower. There is no way to practice cat shots. The first one is the first one. It was memorable and very exhilarating. My subsequent shots were in unison with hooting and hollering, maybe another reason why instructors don't ride along. Once you've finished your required number of traps, you sit on the deck refueling and anxiously waiting for the radio call from the LSO and the magic words: 'You're a qual.' Back on land, we were all very excited and animated. I had been in the Navy for only a year, and flying for only eight months. That night I slept like a baby. The next step was advanced jet training."

Paul Ludwig: "One day when I was flying wing out over the ocean west of Miramar, my engine began making grinding sounds. I asked my section leader to take us home. When we arrived, I wrote up the bad engine. The crew chief refused to believe my write-up because I was the new kid, the most junior officer. I tried to convince him about what I had experienced, and left the ops shack to return to the squadron area. Soon after I got there, the chief phoned me to chew me out, saying I was wrong, that it had only been carburetor icing. Obviously, he didn't want to go to work checking the oil filter on the opinion of a snot-nosed ensign. I was just a kid and he an old chief. My mistake was in not contesting his judgement or challenging his lack of respect. He released the plane for ops without checking the oil filter. The next day a squadron buddy of mine flew that same Skyraider and suffered engine failure on take-off, but managed to get it back on the runway. The filter had metal particles in it. The chief did not apologize for his stupidity."

Demand for the Vought F4U Corsair was so great that Goodyear and Brewster were contracted to help meet it.

Memories

801 Squadron Sea Harrier pilot Peter Wilson aboard the Royal Navy carrier HMS *Illustrious*.

Rear Admiral Dennis Campbell, RN died on 6 April 2000 at the age of ninety-two. His career as a Fleet Air Arm aviator exposed him to many near misses and close calls. He realized early that one of the main dangers to a naval aviator was the liklihood of a collision with parked aircraft, or with a barrier positioned in front of such aircraft to protect them if his plane should fail to catch an arresting cable in his landing. Campbell had a simple, brilliant idea to solve the problem, the angled flight deck. It allowed carrier pilots to approach the deck at a slight angle to the ship itself. If the pilot failed to catch one of the arresting cables, he could "bolt", go around and reenter the landing pattern for another approach by applying full power and flying off the clear port bow. His idea was so effective and

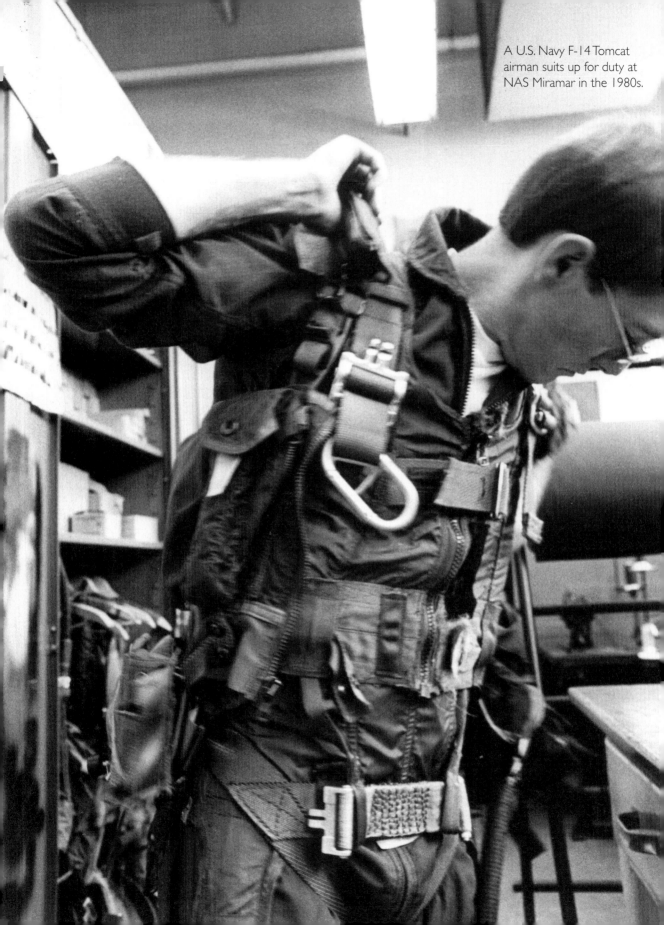

A U.S. Navy F-14 Tomcat airman suits up for duty at NAS Miramar in the 1980s.

successful that both the Royal Navy and the U.S. Navy adopted it quickly and the majority of large aircraft carriers now have an angled flight deck for the recovery of aircraft. Campbell's angled deck concept, and the gyro-stabilized mirror landing system which continously signals glide path corrections to the pilot of a landing aircraft, that pilot is today able to make a precise landing approach on a constant speed and direction, and with a clearly defined escape route should his tailhook fail to engage an arresting cable.

Bill Hannan served on the carrier USS *Kearsarge* in the Korean War as a jet engine mechanic. "It would be difficult to imagine a more hazardous place to live than an aircraft carrier. Apart from the planes landing, and sometimes crashing, on our roof, the ship carried millions of gallons of flammables, including fuel oil, high-octane gasoline, paints, thinner, as well as tons of bombs, rockets and associated ammunition. And scuttlebutt had it that we were being shadowed by submarines.

"Although much of our maintenance work was performed on the hangar deck, some of it was topside under incredibly harrowing conditions. Imagine working on a wintry night, on a frosty deck in rough seas, close to the edge of the ship. Only dim, red-lens flashlights could be used under blackout conditions. If a man happened to slip over the side into the ocean about eighty feet below, there was little chance of him being missed, let alone rescued. Being assigned to plane-pushing meant long hours of physically hard work in particularly dangerous circumstances. Once during my turn on this dreaded duty, I was well forward on the wet flight deck during a launch operation when I was suddenly blown to the deck. I went sliding rapidly towards the propeller planes poised aft with their engines running. I was desperately clawing at the wooden deck, hoping to grab on to one of the numerous metal tie-down strips, when a huge bruiser of a fellow spotted my predicament and, at considerable risk to himself, literally tackled me and dragged me over the edge of the deck into a catwalk. Probably no one else had even seen me. I was speechless and didn't even have a chance to thank him before he rushed back to his post . . . a hero in my view, but probably all in a day's work on the flight deck for him.

"Oral communication was often difficult on the flight deck, even without aircraft engines running. With jet and prop-plane run-ups, it was almost impossible. The ship's powerful 'bull horn' public address system could sometimes be heard over the din, but even in the absence of noise, the bull horn messages were sometimes garbled or distorted like old-time railroad station announcements. So an elaborate system of hand signals evolved that usually worked to make a point.

"The *Kearsarge* converted sea water into fresh quite efficiently, but it had to serve many purposes, the first of which was feeding the ship's thirsty boilers. Conservation measures had to be strictly observed. The shower protocol, for example, was to wet down, turn off the water, soap up, turn on the water, rinse, and turn off the water. Once I had just finished soaping up and was covered with suds, when 'General Quarters' was sounded—loud horns over the intercom system, meaning 'get to your duty station immediately!' I grabbed a pair of shower sandals and my jockey shorts and rushed up to the hangar deck. A 'red alert' was in effect and we could not leave our stations for any reason until the all-clear was sounded. Still covered in soap suds, I was very cold and beginning to itch all over. But it could have been worse. At least I wasn't up on the flight deck.

"Field Days were clean-up times, and meant hard work to anyone involved. The worst thing about them was the closure of the heads (toilet facilities) for cleaning. Time on the ship for 'pit stops' was at a premium there, and often there was little margin for delay in attending to such bodily functions. How frustrating then, after climbing down a deck or two, to find a HEAD SECURED FOR CLEANING sign on the entrance, and either by coincidence or design, any nearby heads were also frequently out of service.

"We headed home at a leisurely pace, probably to reduce wear and tear on the ship's machinery. As keeping idle hands out of mischief was a foremost consideration in the Navy, all sorts of chores, such as chipping paint from decks and then repainting them, were assigned to anyone who appeared to be unoccupied. In our squadron, the most unsavory of our F9F Panthers was selected to have its paint manually stripped, a dirty, tedious job at best, especially when it was freely admitted that the job didn't really need doing."

"Deck landing the Seafire was not too difficult if everything was done properly. The aircraft handled well at low speeds, but I found it necessary to stick my head out over the edge of the cockpit coaming and peering under the exhaust stubs in order to see the batsman's signals. If you handled the aircraft as directed by the batsman, if the batsman gave you the correct signals—as they usually did—and if the flight deck did not duck or dive, then the landing was usually OK. An unreasonable divergence from any of the above criteria would bring the words of the Form 25 (accident report) song to mind: 'The batsman says lower, I always go higher, I drift off to starboard and prang my Seafire, The boys in the goofers all think I am green, But I get my commission from Supermarine.' I flew 200 hours in Seafires and carried out nineteen deck landings without having to sing the song."
—Alan J. Leahy, former Royal Navy fighter pilot

The Hellcat had a kill ratio of nineteen to one; the P-51 Mustang had a kill ratio of fourteen to one; and the Corsair had a kill ratio of eleven to one. Captain Eric Brown flew all the allied and enemy fighters of the war and said that the Hellcat and the Fw 190 were the two best fighters. I never flew the Fw 190, but flew the Hellcat 396 hours in combat. To say I love the Hellcat is an understatement. Only my family do I love more.
—Richard H. May, former U.S. Navy fighter pilot

left: *Illustrious* class British Second World War fleet aircraft carrier *Indomitable*; right: HMS *Illustrious* is dwarfed by the U.S. *Nimitz* class carrier *John C. Stennis*.; upper right: Two views of the Grumman E-2A Hawkeye airborne early warning radar aircraft of the United States Navy.

F6F Hellcat pilots of Fighter Squadron 16 aboard the USS *Lexington* after their successes against Japanese planes near Tarawa on 23 November 1943.

Mass aircraft production was required in the Second World War, a huge and demanding task. Hundreds of thousands of new workers had to be hired and trained. There was little skilled labour available and as time was critical, round-the-clock work shifts were employed. With so many American men away at war, the nation's women had to take up the slack and do much of the work building planes and the other military equipment for the U.S. war effort. American industry produced 150 separate types of aircraft during the war and a total of 300,317 aeroplanes.

left: The Royal Navy's HMS *Illustrious* was the second of three *Invincible* class light aircraft carriers built in the 1970s and 1980s. Participating in Operations Southern Watch in Iraq and Deny Flight in Bosnia, as well as Palliser in Sierra Leone, she also came to the aid of UK citizens trapped by the 2006 Lebanon War. With the retirement of her fixed-wing Sea Harrier aircraft in 2010, she is currently operated as a helicopter carrier and is expected to be withdrawn from active service in 2014. *Illustrious* is shown here with a refuelling vessel; below: Northrop-Grumman EA-6B Prowler; below centre: Boeing F/A-18 Hornet multi-role fighter; bottom: U.S. Marine Corps AV-8B Harrier jump jets.

Royal Navy Sea Harriers
operating on HMS *Illustrious*
in the 1990.s

Catapult crewmen preparing to launch an A-4C Skyhawk from the flight deck of the USS *John F. Kennedy* in 1968.

A Grumman E-2A Hawkeye in the foreground with a Grumman E-1B Tracer alongside, airborne early warning aircraft of the U.S. Navy.